THE JOURNEY FORWARD

THE JOURNEY FORWARD

JAMES SAGAN

Copyright © 2023 by James Sagan.
All Rights Reserved.
No part of this publication may be reproduced, stored in a retrieval system, or transmitted, in any form, or by any means, electronic, mechanical, photocopying, recording, or otherwise, without the prior written consent of the author.

Cover image by permission, artist H. David Wright. "The Spirit of America," © 2009. Images of Eastern Frontiersman; info@davidwrightart.com.

The author has made every effort to ensure that the information in this book was correct at the time of publication, having made concerted effort to accurately document the history of the documents dates, events, locales, and other details through interviews, images, and historical documents. However, the author disclaims any liability caused by errors or omissions, whether errors or omissions result from negligence, accident or any other cause.

Sea-Hill Press (Seahill Inc.), Leesburg, Florida
Website: www.seahillpress.com
Email: info@seahillpress.com
Phone: (877) 397-0005

Ordering Information: Special rates are available on quantity purchases.
For details, please direct inquiries to orders@seahillpress.com.

ISBN: 9798218207793

Printed in the United States of America.

CONTENTS

INTRODUCTION VII
THE ROBINSON NAME 1
THE FAMILY 3
THE JOURNEY PART 1 5
    Key Elements of Survival 7
    Immigrants to British America 8
THE AMERICAN REVOLUTIONARY WAR 13
THE JOURNEY PART 2 27
THE BIG SEWICKLEY SETTLEMENT 33
THEIR STORIES 41
    Robert Sr. & Isabella 43
    William & Jane 45
    Robert Jr. & Rachel 55
    John & Margaret 65
    Jennie & Thomas 93
    Lavina & Samuel 95
        The Whiskey Rebellion and Samuel Weir 98
LIFE ON THE FRONTIER 113
THE ROBINSON STRONG HOUSE 123
A JOURNEY COMPLETED 127
EPILOGUE 135

INTRODUCTION

It's often said that genealogical research is the second most popular hobby in the United States after gardening. In our family, genealogical research of my maternal ancestors, the Robinson lineage, was ranked lower on the popularity list. Way lower. In fact, you could say it didn't even make the list because there was never anything to find, according to our mother. Knowing the names and general towns of birth of our maternal grandparents were sufficient.

Decades later my brother, Jim Sagan, dabbled in the genealogy of his partner's father of British birth. The childhood stories of "Bertie," as told by Diane's father, were actually his World War II adventures. My brother suspected more to the stories and unveiled "Bertie" was likely a British spy. The exciting bedtime stories explained Diane's father's absences from home and family.

Intrigued by our own grandfather's military service, the search for information relating to his Army service or his life before and after World War I was relatively unproductive. Our mother was right. There was not much information to find regarding the ancestors of Joseph Robinson, our grandfather. However, a lost and forgotten document amongst files changed everything we knew about our Robinson lineage. A rich family history encompassing many American historical events emerged from the research. These facts about the lives of our ancestors tell a story not only of our family history but of American history as well. Consequently, the Robinson legacy and place in American history fills the following pages of this book.

I will humbly admit that the newest hobby in both my brother's and my home has become genealogical research. Needless to say, our gardens have, consequently, suffered!

Nancy L (Sagan) Summers

THE ROBINSON NAME

Robinson is one of the most interesting and evocative surnames of the British Isles, whilst being recorded throughout the English-speaking world. It is a medieval patronymic from a given name of Robin, itself a diminutive of the popular Anglo-Saxon pre-seventh-century personal name Robert.

This was originally a compound name with the elements "hrothl" and "bertha," meaning "fame-bright." As such, it is first recorded in England in the famous Domesday Book of 1086. It is said that the name was originally made popular by Robin Goodfellow, whose mischievous tricks were later described in Shakespeare's *Midsummer Night's Dream*, and perhaps even more so by Robin of Locksley, otherwise known as Robin Hood, who it is said (without too much evidence) stole from the rich to give to the poor.

The surname was first recorded in the latter half of the thirteenth century, and Margaret Robines appeared in the Hundred Rolls of Cambridgeshire, dated 1279. Recordings from early surviving church registers include the marriage of Helen Robinson and Thomas Grene on October 1, 1548, at St. Leonard's Eastcheap, and the marriage of Christopher Robinson and Jone Millman on November 4, 1585, at St. Mary Abchurch, London.

An early settler in the New World Colonies was John Robinson, age twenty-eight, who sailed from London on the ship *Peter Bonaventure*, bound for Barbados in April 1635. The Coat of Arms most associated with the name is a green shield charged with gold chevron between three gold bucks standing at the gaze. The first recorded spelling of the family name is shown to be that of Dere Robins, which is dated 1273, in the Hundred Rolls of Cambridgeshire.

Through the centuries, surnames in every country have continued to develop, often leading to astonishing variants of the original spelling.

- » An English and Scottish name, and a form in the name of Robin, as well as referring to the son of Robert.
- » Various spellings include Robins, Robbings, Robison, Robertson, Robens, and Robyns.
- » In the United States, most with the Robinson surname live in Virginia, Pennsylvania, New York, Texas, Illinois, and Ohio. It is a popular surname in England, Canada, Australia, and Scotland. In Ireland around the area of Ulster, the Robinson surname is a frequently found surname.

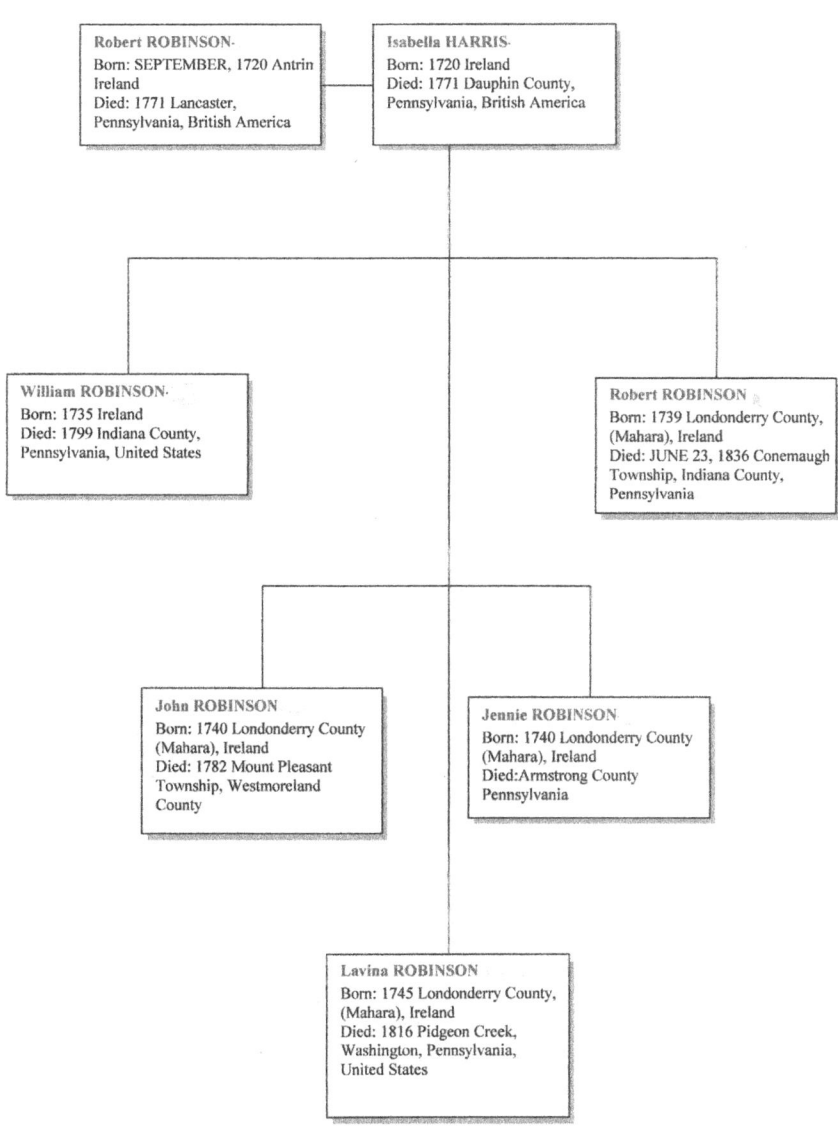

Robert Robinson Sr. Family Chart

THE JOURNEY
PART 1

THIS IS THE STORY OF THE ROBINSON FAMILY AND THEIR JOURNEY IN AMERICA. This story details the experiences of a brave and broad-minded family who first crossed an ocean and then raging rivers, chopped down forests, plowed miles of land, suffered incalculable hardships, and braved a lonely frontier to forge a new American ideal.

These settlers were drawn to British America for many reasons including religious freedom, opportunities to own land, and to make money through trade. While the population in British America tended to remain along the eastern seaboard, it was only a matter of time until the population growth would push settlement to the west into lands inhabited by Native Americans. This story is a uniquely American story of people whose ambition and courage led them to remarkable accomplishments and to establish their legacy.

The journey to British America for the Robinson family follows the paths of those Irish immigrants before them. Perhaps several factors were behind this decision to leave Ireland. First, Presbyterians and Catholics were targeted by Ireland's laws, whereas the Presbyterians had no political power, and the Catholics could not own any land. Next, there was the famine in the 1740s that killed more than 400,000 people in Ireland.

In the 1770s and 1780s most Scots-Irish landed in Philadelphia, Pennsylvania. They moved up to the Delaware River to Bucks County and then up the Susquehanna and Cumberland Valleys, finding the flat lands along the rivers and creeks to set up their log cabins, their grist mills, and their Presbyterian churches in Chester, Lancaster, and Dauphin counties. These areas became their strongholds, and they built towns such as

Chambersburg, Gettysburg, Carlisle, and York. Then, the next generation moved into western Pennsylvania.

Without much cash, they moved to the free lands on the frontier, becoming the typical western "squatters," as the frontier guard of the colony, on what the historian Frederick Jackson Turner described as "the cutting edge of the frontier."

Evidently, this would be the path that the Robinson family would follow.

This journey for the Robinson's began when John Robinson, the youngest son of Robert Robinson Sr. and Isabella Harris Robinson, decided to travel to British America to be with his future wife, Margaret Jameson. John would become the trailblazer to British America for the Robinson family.

Then in early 1770, John Robinson would return to Maghera, Londonderry County, Northern Ireland *(see image, below)*, to escort and guide the largest group of the family members on their journey to British America. The Robinson family was leaving for British America.

Maghera, Londonderry County
Maghera is a small town at the foot of the Glenshane Pass in County Londonderry, Northern Ireland. Maghera (pronounced MAH-he-RAH) is from Machaire Ratha, meaning "plain of the ringfort."

John Robinson escorted the first family group to immigrate to British America, which included his brother Robert Robinson Jr. and his wife, Rachel. Along with them were his youngest sister, Lavina, and her husband, Samuel Weir, and their children. They traveled on the ship called the *Phoenix*, captained by James Mitchell. The *Phoenix* departed from Londonderry, Ireland, and arrived in Philadelphia on Wednesday July 25, 1770. There were eighty-five passengers aboard the *Phoenix*.

Also, on the ship were eighteen other members of the Weir family, including Samuel Weir's brother and sister. Most of the Weir family members would eventually settle in Virginia.

After their arrival, the families then traveled west on the Great Conestoga Road from Philadelphia to Lancaster County, Pennsylvania. Like most of the early roads, the Conestoga Road followed old Indian trails through the wilderness. Over these roads they pushed their way westward on what the Native Americans had named "Conestoga," which means "Great Magic Land." They crossed the Schuylkill River by ferry to get to Lancaster County.

Shortly after arriving, on September 5, 1770, Robert and Rachel's first child, a daughter named Martha, was born in Marietta, Lancaster County, Pennsylvania.

KEY ELEMENTS OF SURVIVAL

These immigrants relied upon three very important elements of survival that during those times. First, they were always willing to work and do anything to make money, as evidenced throughout this story.

Second, like most families emigrating for British America at the time, the family members stayed together from the time they arrived in Philadelphia until they arrived on the western frontier of Pennsylvania, as evidenced in this quote about the Robinson family: *"These families remained near each other, tarrying to Lancaster and Dauphin counties, finally proceeding to Big Sewickley, Westmoreland County."* [1]

Third, as was described earlier and typical of this time, one of the sons, John Robinson, was sent to British America prior to the arrival of the rest of the family to obtain land so that the other family members would have a place to settle.

IMMIGRANTS TO BRITISH AMERICA

During the next several years while living in Lancaster County, Robert and Rachel's family grew to a family of six. They and their children—Martha, John, Betsy, and James—continued to live in Mount Joy Township, Pennsylvania. His brother William Robinson, along with sister Lavina Robinson Weir, brother-in-law Samuel Weir, and their children also lived nearby in Mount Joy Township.

Although they did not travel together, these family members eventually made it to British America in the 1770 to 1771 time period:

First immigrant, 1766, at age twenty-six:
- **John Robinson** (third son of Robert Sr. and Isabella)

Second immigrant group, arrived June 21, 1770:
- **William Robinson** (oldest of Robert Sr. and Isabella)
- **William Robinson Jr.**, his son (Note: William Jr. died shortly after their arrival in America.)

Third immigrant group, escorted by John, arrived July 25, 1770:
- **Robert Robinson Jr.** (second son of Robert Sr. and Isabella) and **Rachel Weir**, his wife, (sister of Samuel Weir)
- **Lavina Robinson Weir** (nicknamed Levy, and the youngest daughter of Robert Sr. and Isabella), her husband, **Samuel Israel Weir Sr.**, and their four children at the time, **Jane, Thomas, Elisabeth, and James Weir**
  (See actual passenger list, pp. 10–11)

Fourth immigrant group, arrived October 25, 1771:
- **Robert Robinson Sr.**, patriarch, and his wife (matriarch), **Isabella Harris Robinson**
- **Jennie Robinson** (oldest daughter of Robert Sr. and Isabella; twin of John Robinson)

Later immigrants, William's family:
- **James** (son), departed from London on March 6, 1772
- **John** (son) arrived in Philadelphia on March 1, 1773
- **Samuel** (son), departed from London in January 1774
- **Jane** (wife), arrived in Philadelphia in January 1774

Upon arrival in Lancaster County, Pennsylvania, and during the period of 1770–1771, Robert Robinson Jr. worked as a mason on the John Harris House (today called the Cameron House) in Harrisburg, Pennsylvania. Robert and Rachel lived in Marietta, Lancaster County, which was approximately twenty-five to thirty miles from Harrisburg, Pennsylvania. The work on the house started in 1766, and the house was frequently extended and altered over the years. It stands today as a two-and-a-half story Georgian-style house of mortared limestone.

The map of Lancaster County, Pennsylvania, *(see map, p. 12)* shows the location of Marietta *(Key 2. Marietta; circled)*, where Robert and Rachel's first daughter, Martha, was born; also, it shows the location of Mount Joy Township in Lancaster County, Pennsylvania, *(circled)* where the Robinsons lived for several years.

With the money Robert Jr. earned working on the John Harris House as a mason, he purchased 150 acres of land in Mount Joy Township, Lancaster County, Pennsylvania, in 1771.

The John Harris House (Cameron House) in Harrisburg, Pennsylvania

1770	Ships Names	Masters Names	From whence	Passengers Names
July 25	Ship Manny	James Mitchell	Londonderry	And¹ White
Robt Queen
Jn⁰ McDaniel
Nich Henley
Joseph Bedson
Barney Coney
Bridg¹ D⁰
Tho⁵ Maguire
W⁰ Moore
John Moor
James Norris
Jn⁰ Roney
W⁰ Ledley
Tho⁵ McCurdy
Jn⁰ Lieb
W⁰ M⁵auter
Jn⁰ Dougal
James Coag
Mary Coag
Moses Rowley
Joseph Hunter
Jn⁰ Dougan
W⁰ Liney
Tho⁵ Adams
Robt Mess
Lucy Mess
Tho⁵ Mess
Peg Mess
Mary Mess
August 4	Snow Amelia	Gideon Villineufre	London	M⁵ Hillard
D⁰ Drummond
2 Dublaer

10

Phoenix Passenger List, July 25, 1770 [2]
Thomas Cadwalader, Cadwalader genealogical collection, "Passenger Lists, with Duties, August 29, 1768, to May 13, 1772,"

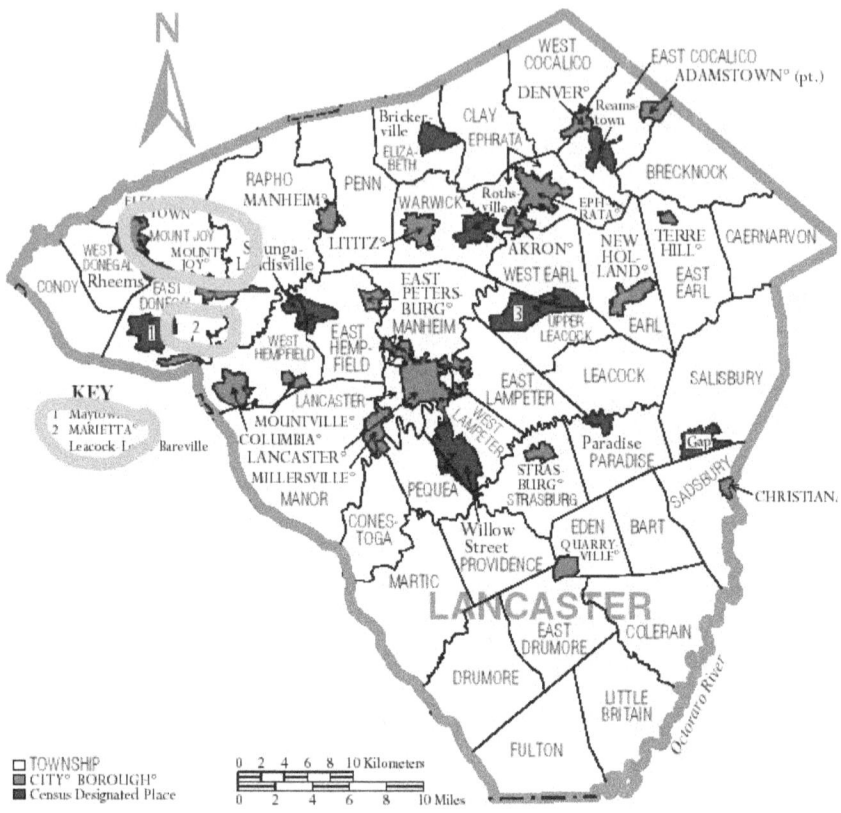

Map of Lancaster County, Pennsylvania, with Municipal and Township Labels
Pennsylvania Proprietary and State Tax Lists of the County of Lancaster for the years 1771, 1772, and 1773 show that Robert Robinson had a farm in Mount Joy Township of 150 acres with two horses and two cattle. He paid a tax of 12 pounds and 6 pence for 1771 and 1772, but on 12 pounds for 1773.

THE AMERICAN REVOLUTIONARY WAR

In March 1777, the Pennsylvania Militia Law was in effect. The law stated that all white males between the ages of seventeen and fifty-three were automatically enrolled in the militia.

According to this law, and for purposes of administration and drill, companies and battalions of militia were set up on a geographical basis. The draft was instituted upon a class roll. That is that each county was to establish eight battalion districts. These districts could encompass a handful of townships within the county, especially if there were several smaller townships with lower populations. Everyone who met the draft criteria was given a class number between 1 and 8. Depending on the need, one or more classes could be called up at any given time to serve.

When the classes were called up, each captain would deliver a notice to each man's dwelling or place of business. The names of those who turned out for muster duty would then appear on company muster rolls. Some of these muster rolls provide the date of when duty began, and in the case of officers, the date of their commission. The men in each battalion elected their own officers, and those from each company chose their company officers. In 1777, all eight classes of the Lancaster County Militia were called up. They would then serve two months active service. Active service, when it occurred, would have been for sixty days at a time.[3]

The Militia Law forced a difficult choice on all Pennsylvanians. Each person had to weigh the cost benefits of showing up for an exercise drill, a muster, and service against paying a steep fine. There was a concern that a County Lieutenant would force someone's family member to service in their stead, and danger was very real in the wilderness. For some, serving

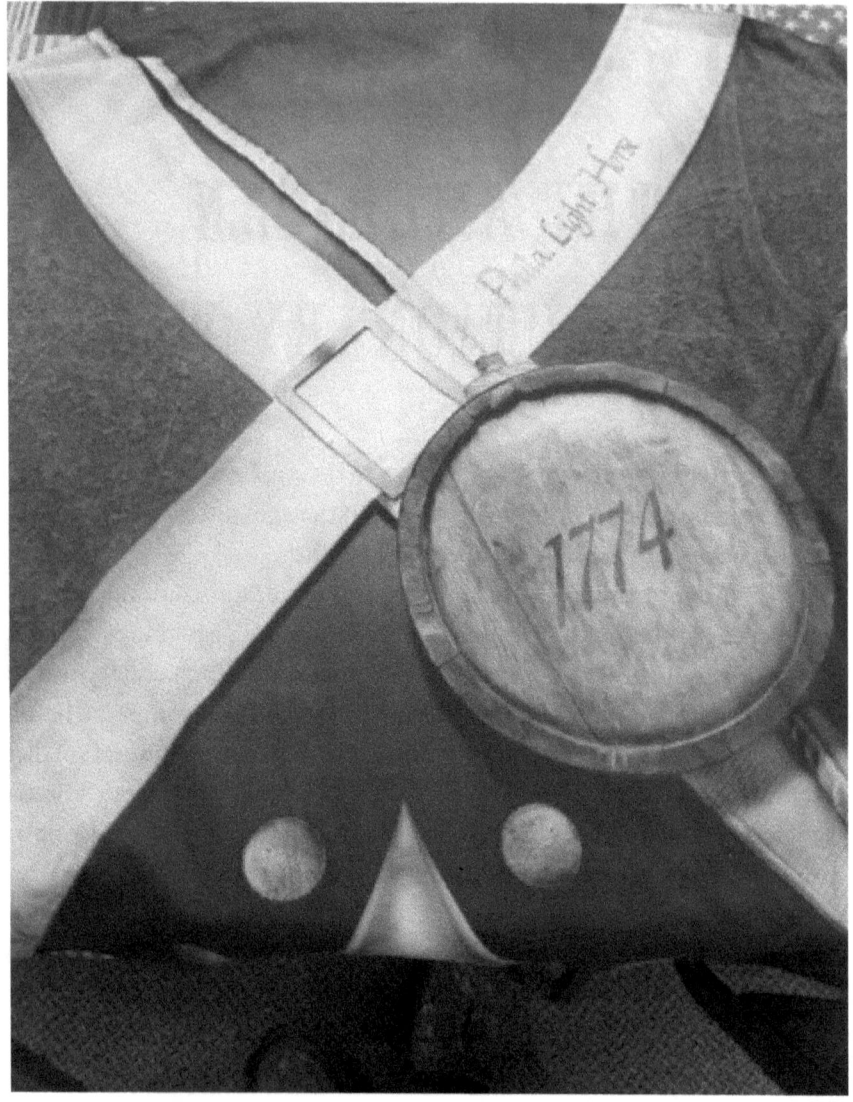

First Troop Philadelphia City Cavalry, or "First City Troop"
Organized in 1774 as the Light Horse of the City of Philadelphia, or Phila Light Horse.

WE THE DESCENDANTS OF THE AMERICAN REVOLUTION WHO, BY THEIR SACRIFICES, ESTABLISHED THE UNITED STATES OF AMERICA, REAFFIRM OUR FAITH IN THE PRINCIPLES OF LIBERTY, OUR CONSTITUTIONAL REPUBLIC, AND SOLEMNLY PLEDGE OURSELVES TO DEFEND THEM AGAINST EVERY FOE.

(Pledge of the Sons of American Revolution)

tours and showing up for exercises was not worth risking the death of their crops. Regardless of what they decided, there were serious consequences.[4]

Most of the service rendered by members of the Pennsylvania Militia fell into one of three categories: (1) They were used to augment the operations of the Continental Line. (2) Large numbers of Pennsylvania militia were employed in the summer and autumn of 1777 to oppose the British invasion of Brandywine and on the flanks at the battle of Germantown, though in neither case did they see any action. Due to the sixty-day turnover, none of the men that were at Brandywine in September would have been present at Whitemarsh in December. (3) This type of service was duty on the frontier in Northumberland, Northampton, Bedford, and Westmoreland Counties. Occasionally, militia reinforcements from Cumberland, Lancaster, and York counties would be brought in to reinforce these frontiers as occurred in the summer of 1778.[5]

+++

Samuel Weir (husband of Lavina Robinson Weir) and the three Robinson brothers served during the Revolutionary War.

By mid-year of 1777, Samuel, William Robinson, and Robert Robinson decided to serve in the Lancaster County Militia. Even though Robert, William, and Samuel were in the Lancaster County Militia, they were in different battalions and companies of the militia.

Their younger brother, John, served as a Frontier Ranger in Westmoreland County, Pennsylvania.

SAMUEL WEIR

On July 31, 1777, while living in Lancaster County, Pennsylvania, Samuel Weir was commissioned a First Lieutenant in the 5th Company (Captain Patrick Hayes), 6th Battalion, Lancaster County Militia. He was thirty-seven years old at the time of his commission.[6]

After his service in the Lancaster County Militia, and later after moving to Washington County, Pennsylvania, Samuel also served as Private in Capt. Crawford's Company of the Washington County Militia in the Seventh Class in October 1781.

COMMONWEALTH OF PENNSYLVANIA
PENNSYLVANIA HISTORICAL AND MUSEUM COMMISSION
BUREAU OF ARCHIVES AND HISTORY
WILLIAM PENN MEMORIAL MUSEUM AND ARCHIVES BUILDING
BOX 1026
HARRISBURG, PENNSYLVANIA 17108

February 13, 1973

TO WHOM IT MAY CONCERN:

This is to certify that one S A M U E L   W I E R was commissioned July 31, 1777 as a First Lieutenant, Fifth Company (Captain Hays), Sixth Battalion, Lancaster County Militia, according to the evidence of an undated Return of Officers of the Sixth Battalion.

HARRY E. WHIPKEY, Chief
Division of Archives & Manuscripts

Authority: Military Returns (Militia), Records of the Comptroller General, at the Division of Archives & Manuscripts

Residence ascribed: Londonderry Township

Samuel Weir, Certified Lancaster Militia Record

```
                                                    Inactive Duty
                                                         Militia
    WEIR, SAMUEL                           Rank  PVT.
Lieutenancy  WASHINGTON              County.  Battalion   5TH
Company   1ST                                  Class      7TH
Remarks:
Authority:  C/R
             Nov. 2, 1781                          A (6), II, 148
Date                     Muster Fines £    Published
"Military Accounts: Militia," Records of the Comptroller General, RG-4
       THE BASIC RECORD DOES NOT PROVE ACTIVE DUTY.
```

Samuel Weir, Washington County Militia Record

He was one of the three men of the Washington County Militia, who along with his brother-in-law Robert Robinson, that was on the payroll as a guard to the commissioners to run a temporary line between the states of Pennsylvania and Virginia, commencing September 28, 1781, and ending October 5, 1781, during the War of the Revolution.

His Washington County military service ended on November 2, 1781.[7]

WILLIAM ROBINSON

William was Private in the First Class of the 4th Company, 6th Battalion, Lancaster County Militia (commanded by Colonel James Taylor), in 1777. He took the Oath of Allegiance in Lancaster County on July 2, 1777. He was forty-two years old at the time.

After taking the Oath of Allegiance, William joined the Revolutionary War effort.[8]

```
AND MILITIA OF THE REVOLUTION.      453

NAMES OF PERSONS WHO TOOK THE OATH OF AL-
  LEGIANCE TO THE STATE OF PENNSYLVANIA IN
  LANCASTER TOWNSHIP, 1777.

                    July 2, 1777.
Andrew Heikis.            Samuel Caughey.
Jacob Hagestwiler.        Thomas Palmer.
Jacob Geiger.             Jacob Foltz.
Leonard Shubler.          Charles Herre.
John Mitchel.             John Harris.
Valentine Hoffman.        John Miller.
Malcom McCune.            William McConnell.
Robert Calbraith.         Robert Evan.
John Posley.              George McCune.
John Anderson.            William Dunlap.
Joseph Craford.           William Tens.
Robert Elder.             James Crage.
Robert Anderson.          Hugh Coming.
James McKneely.           Alexander Huston.
Alexander Morrison.       Samuel Entriken.
Richard Free.             Alexander May.
Alexander Russell.        Captain Joseph Anderson.
Hugh Pussly.              Robert Miller.
Robert Andrews.           Andrew Russell.
Thomas Anderson.          William Downing, Jr.
Daniel McCredy.           John Crage.
Hugh McCasland.           Thomas Scott.
John Coming.              John Andrews.
Henry Potter.             John Crage, Jr.
John Scott.               James McKnight.
Gabriel Morrison.         John Gill.
Alexander Hasson.         James Finley.
James Tease.              John Baird.
Andrew McGinniss.         Samuel McCalmont.
William Robinson.         Samuel Moore.
Robert Ross.              James Walker,
James Calbreath.          Duncan Kinnan.
Thomas Dick.              Samuel Gill.
Samuel Galbraith.         George McCartney.
Alexander Speer.          James Mckindry.
Samuel Caughey.           Thomas Willson.
William McConnel.         John Patterson.
John Rowe.                Hugh Willson.
```

William Robinson, Oath of Allegiance, 1777

ROBERT ROBINSON JR.

Robert was called up (he was in the first class) in 1777 and elected by the company as a First Lieutenant for the 3rd Battalion, 2nd Company of the Lancaster County Militia from Mount Joy Township under Capt. Thomas Robinson. He took the Oath of Allegiance on September 5, 1777, in Lancaster County. He was thirty-eight years old at the time. By May 1778, Robert was listed as Inactive Military Duty.

It is possible that Capt. Thomas Robinson and Robert Robinson knew each other. Their fathers emigrated from the same area in Ireland. The Thomas Robinson family lived in Delaware, and that was where he was born in 1751. This was Thomas Robinson's first command, at the age twenty-six. He was in the Continental Army prior to this command but did not go with his unit to the Canadian Campaign due to sickness. It is possible that Thomas Robinson selected or chose (not commissioned) to make Robert a First Lieutenant because he knew Robert and needed someone older and trustworthy to help keep the other soldiers in line. By the time of the 1781 muster roll, Robert Robinson was listed as Private (Inactive Duty) on the Muster Roll of April 23, 1781.

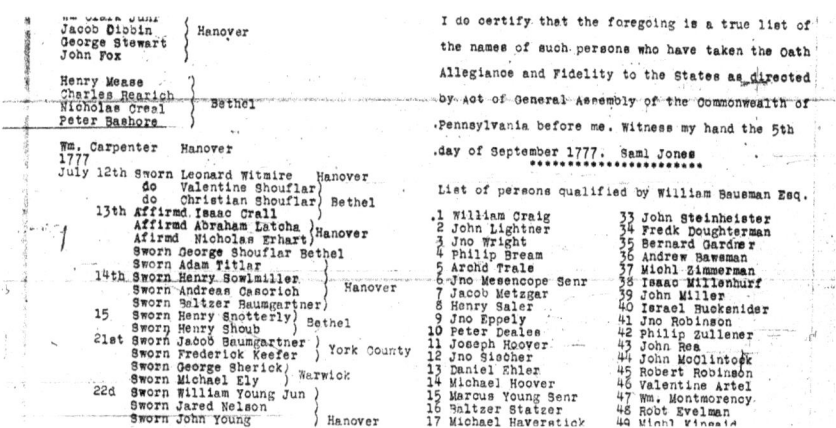

Robert Robinson, Oath of Allegiance and Fidelity, 1777
Robert Robinson is listed as number 45

On the April 20, 1778, Muster Roll *(shown below)*, Robert Robinson is listed as First Lieutenant in Capt. Thomas Robinson's Mount Joy Township First Class Militia Muster Roll.[9]

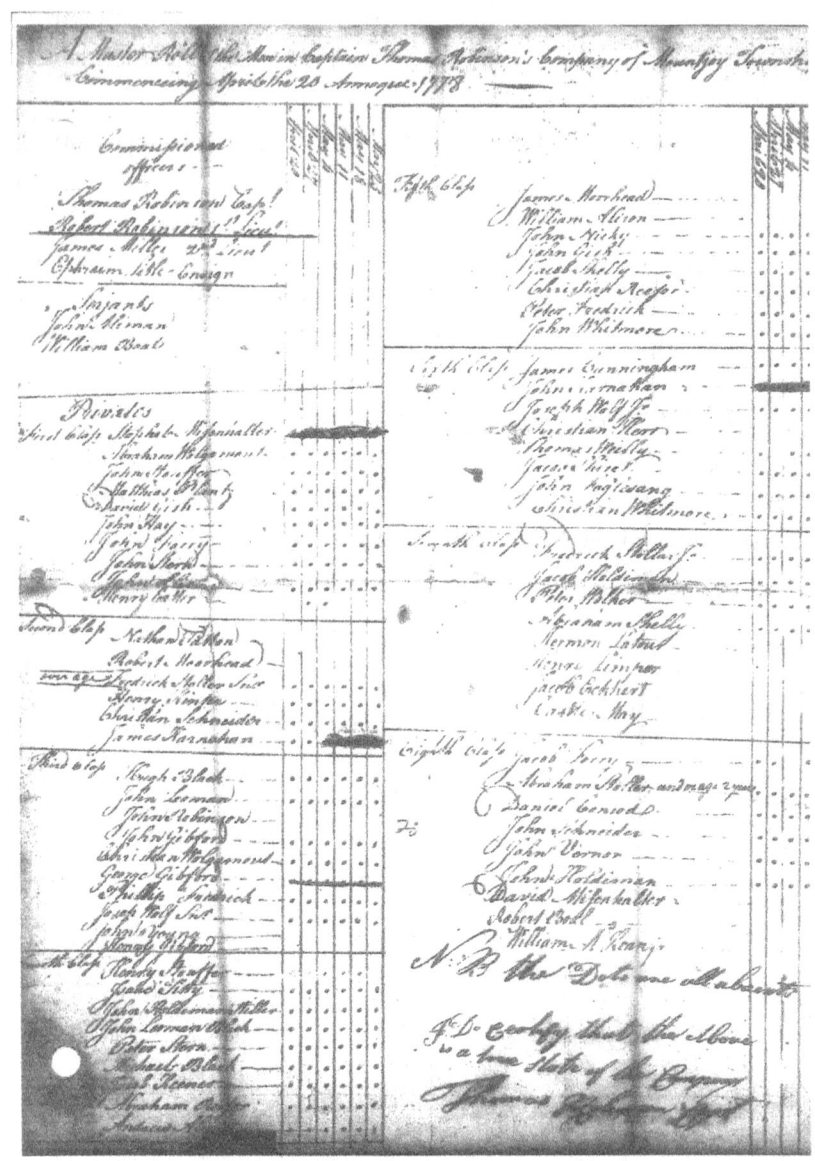

Robert Robinson, April 1778, Original Muster Roll

Robert Robinson, First Lieutenant

Capt. Robert Robinson, Military Index Card, Lancaster County, 1778

Robert Robinson was also a Frontier Ranger from 1778 to 1783. He served as a private in Captain Eleazer Williamson's Company in Westmoreland County, Pennsylvania, during the Revolutionary War.

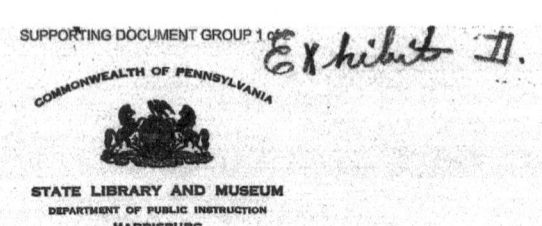

Robert Robinson, Frontier Ranger Certificate

JOHN ROBINSON

In 1778, John Robinson fulfilled his patriotic duty by serving as a Frontier Ranger in Westmoreland County *(see "Rangers on the Frontiers" list, p. 24)*.[10] John took the Oath of Allegiance in Westmoreland County, Pennsylvania, on October 3, 1777, before Hugh Martin, Esq. John was thirty-three years old at the time.

```
36                OATH OF ALLEGIANCE

      The Names of Those that Have Taken the Oath of Fidelity
      Before Me, Together with the Years, Months and Days of the
      Months when Taken, pr. Me, HUGH MARTIN, Esq.
      September ye 11, 1777.  SAMUEL GLASGOW.
                         23,  JOHN GIFFIN.
                         23,  MOSES LOTTA.
                         23,  SAMUEL ROBINSON.
                         23,  ALEXANDER MAXWELL.
                         23,  SAMUEL SERRELS.
                         24,  ISAAC MILLER.
                         26,  JACOB McCLAIN.
      October ye   3, 1777.   ISAAC McHENDRY.
                          3,  JOSEPH HUTCHISON.
                          9,  CLEMENTS McGERRY.
                          9,  JOSEPH EAGER.
                          9,  WILLIAM ROBINSON.
                          9,  JAMES McQUISTON.
                          9,  JOHN KILGORE.
                         10,  GEORGE LATIMER.
                         13,  ROBERT WADDLE.
                         13,  JOHN ROBINSON.
```

John Robinson, Oath of Allegiance, October 13, 1777

224   RANGERS ON THE FRONTIERS—1778-1783.

Sam'l Ralston.
John Fitch.
Thomas Hughes.
Thomas Lyon.
Thomas Colhoon.
William Sell.
Dennis Springer, Lieut.
Hugh Goudey, Ensign.
Thomas Moore, Capt.
John Lawson.
Joseph Rodgers.
William Moore.
Jerrit Regin.
Charles May.
Daniel Mathews.
William Jones.
Jacob Hauseman.
Butler Case.
Thomas Lyon.
Joseph Lenrow.
Frederick Rhoades.
Edward Mitchell.
Elijah Hart.
William Mathew.
John Thomson.
William Sells.
Samuel Ralston.
Obediah Robins.
Stephen Kitchens.
Rob't Applegate.
John Applegate.
Benj. Applegate.
Benj. Sparks.
Richard Sparks.
Christopher Haydon.
James Chambers.
Rob't McGill.
Rob't Mitchell.
Archibald Leech, Lieut.
Archibald McCallaster.
Wm. Dunlop.
James Glasgow.
Wm. Clark.
Ralph Cherry.
Wm. Young.

Jn'o Thompson.
Andrew Johnson.
Daniel Kirkpatrick.
Henry Fulton.
Robert Fulton.
Wm. Caldwell.
Archibald Leech.
John Bell.
John Kirkpatrick.
Wm. Hall.
James Carroll.
Archibald Fields.
James Bennefield.
Wm. Espy.
John Henry.
John Haddey.
Wm. Ownes.
Thomas McGraw.
Andrew Stewart.
John Maguire.
James Hutchison.
Jn'o Johnston.
Jn'o Gordon.
Henry Rardin.
George Biddle.
Jn'o Mollender.
David Mellender.
Christ'n Dear.
Peter Dear.
Rob't McDowell.
Jesse Stewart.
James Piper.
Campbell Lefeve.
John Robinson.
John Rose.
Hugh McKinney.
Aaron Chinney.
Sam'l Sellers.
Reuben Kemp, Capt.
James Alexander.
Malachi Sutton.
David Hathaway.
Joseph Vankirk.
John Barker.

John Robinson, Ranger Service

In 1777, the commanding officer of the Lancaster County battalions was Colonel Alexander Lowery. In early September, all the Lancaster battalions of Col. Lowery were hurried on and fought in the Battle of Brandywine on September 11th to protect the left flank of George Washington's Continental Army at Pyle Fork. The battalions escaped the battle as shown on the lower left corner on the following map of the battle. Capt. Thomas Robinson, Robert's commanding officer, was wounded in this battle.

After the battle of Brandywine, the Lancaster County battalions of Lowery were responsible for protecting the flank of the Continental Army at the Battle of Germantown on October 4, 1777.[11]

The sixty-day militia service of Robert, William, and Samuel would have included these historical battles, and they would have been back on their plantations before the harsh winter began. It should be noted that none of the militias that participated in the Battle of Brandywine were at the camp at Valley Forge during the brutal winter in December 1777.

Robert, William, and Samuel served their sixty-day commitment and returned home thereafter.

Sons of the American Revolution Military Medal, *Libertas Et Patria*

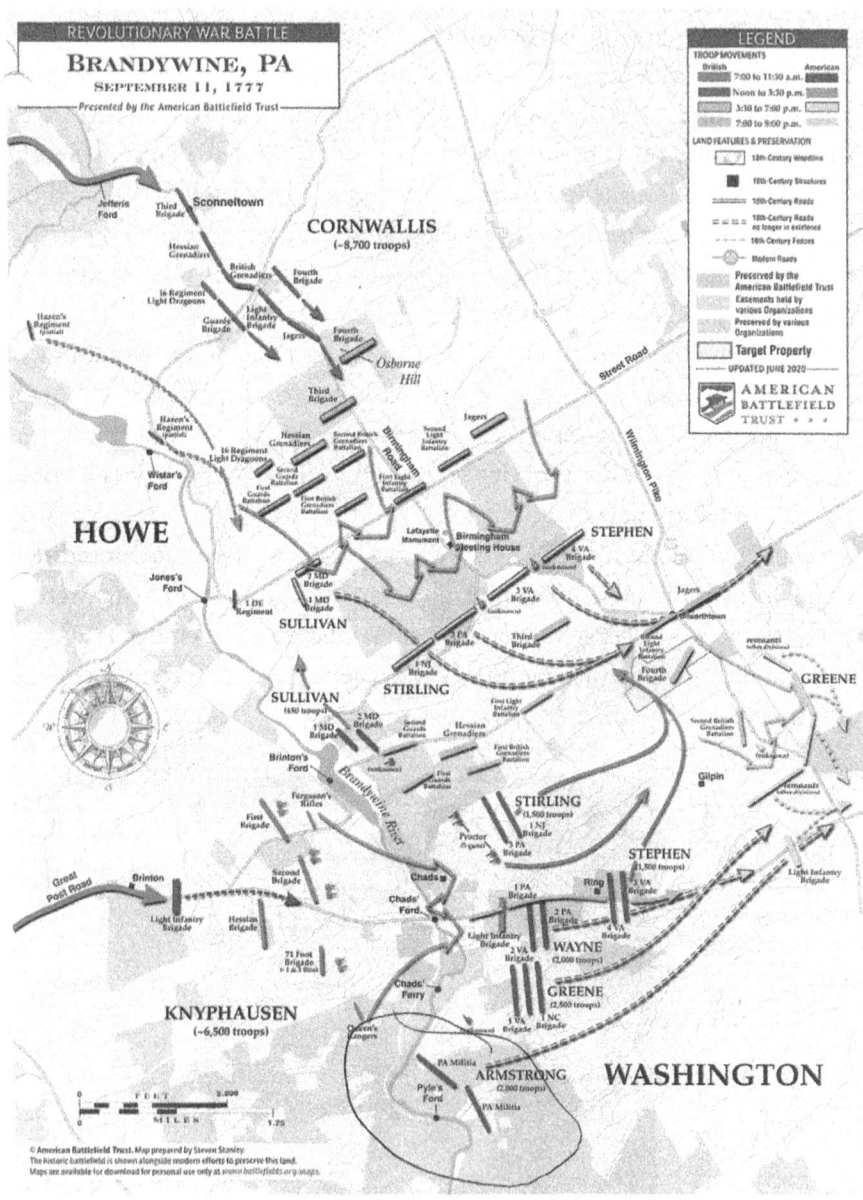

Battle of Brandywine Map[12]

THE JOURNEY PART 2

After Robert, William, and Samuel completed militia service in late 1777, the families decided that the war was too close, and so to protect their families they should find new homes on the western frontier. They would join their brother John at the Big Sewickley Settlement in Mount Pleasant Township, Westmoreland County, Pennsylvania.

The first step toward moving to the western frontier was for everyone to sell their plantations in Lancaster County, Pennsylvania, and move to the Conocoheague (Conikakig) Settlement in Franklin County. This settlement was one of the largest settlements of Scottish and Irish immigrants in Pennsylvania at the time. Once there, they would join other Scottish and Irish settlers and form a wagon train to travel to the western frontier.

The families sold their plantations in late 1777 and early 1778 and moved to the Conocoheague (Conikakig) Settlement in Franklin County, Pennsylvania. While there, Robert helped construct a mill for the settlement. This is another example of how Robert worked during the journey to make money to obtain a future for his family.

+++

Almost all the people living in this area east of the Appalachian Mountains were landowning farmers. They raised the food they needed for their own consumption and sold or traded the rest for items they could not grow or make (such as coffee, sugar, and shoes). In large communities like the Conocoheague Settlement, people tended to specialize in making a particular item (such as soap, candles, boots, wooden utensils, or straw brooms). They would trade their specialty product for other goods.

A typical family had six or seven members living at home. The farmhouse was made of wood planks and had two stories and an average of four rooms. In addition to the house, there was a barn, a cellar for food storage, and an outhouse. Farms had varying amounts of acreage, but almost all had a vegetable garden close to the house and corn or wheat planted on the land beyond the house. Corn was planted the first few years. As the soil became less fertile after numerous plantings, most farmers turned to wheat, which did not require very rich soil. Cows, pigs, chickens, and sheep were raised for milk, meat, eggs, and wool.

A typical central town within a farming region had neat two-story houses along a central road, a church or two, a school, a meeting hall, and stores. Sawmills and gristmills for grinding corn and wheat were in each community. Roads and canals made trade between the communities easier. With all these conveniences, rural Americans living east of the Appalachians had an easier lifestyle than settlers on the west side of the mountains.

+++

By mid-year of 1778, Robert and Rachel, and their family of Martha (age eight), John (age six), Elizabeth (age three), and James (age one)—along with Robert's brother William, his sister Jennie and husband Thomas Smith, his sister Lavina and husband Samuel and their family of seven children—all traveled west on the Forbes Road from the Conocoheague Creek Settlement in Franklin County headed to an area called the Big Sewickley Settlement on the western frontier *(see map, p. 29)*. However, at this time, William's wife, Jane, and their sons—Samuel, James, John, and Robert—did not want to make the journey and live on the frontier. They elected to stay at the Conococheague Settlement until 1789–1790.

+++

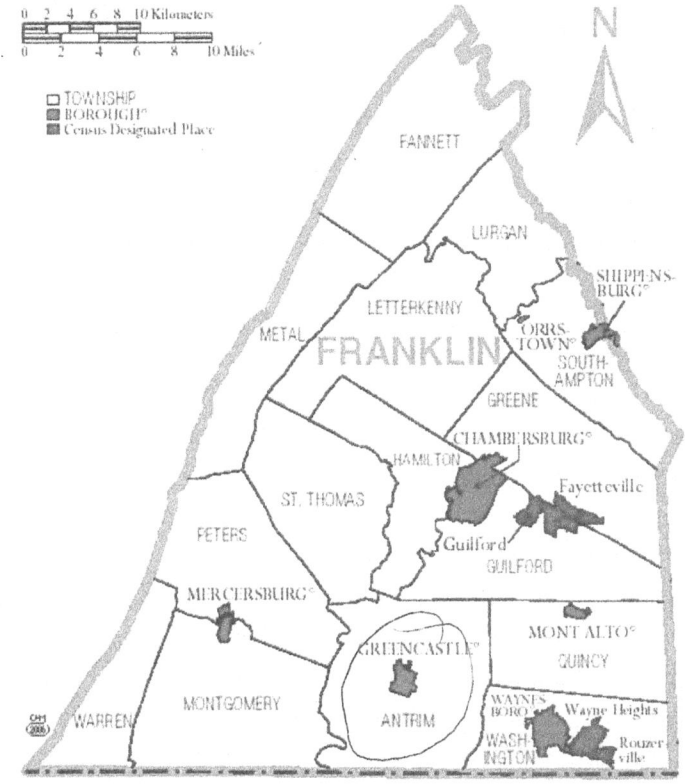

Franklin County Map

This map shows the approximate location of the Conocoheague (Conokakig) Settlement. In 1735, Jacob Snively, James Johnston, Joseph Crunkelton, and James Rody made their "Conocoheague Settlement" a few miles away from the present location of Greencastle, Pennsylvania. Other people soon followed them, and in 1741, the court in Lancaster, Pennsylvania, accepted their application for township status. The township is named for Antrim, Ireland, which indicates that the first residents were of Scots-Irish heritage. Antrim contains one borough (Greencastle) and six villages.

The Pennsylvania Trail was the first great road across the Alleghenies in Pennsylvania. The initial section of this migratory path opened in 1755 and ran from Harrisburg through Shippensburg to the summit of the Allegheny Ridge. This road was the principal route used by early settlers as they moved west beyond the Susquehanna River to what are now Franklin, Fulton, and Bedford Counties.

The western section of the Pennsylvania Trail is also known as Forbes Road *(see map, p. 31)*. The Forbes Road began a westward push from Carlisle through Shippensburg and Chambersburg to Raystown (now Bedford), Pennsylvania. From here, a wagon road was cut over the Allegheny Mountains into the trackless wilderness of western Pennsylvania. Much of this route traversed the Native Americans "Raystown Path" to about ten miles west of Ligonier. During the construction of the Forbes Road, a series of fortifications such as Fort Loudon, Fort Littleton, Fort Bedford, and Fort Ligonier were built to serve as supply depots.

In 1758, during the French and Indian War, this trans-mountain road was widened to provide passage for General Forbes's wagon trains. This migration route was utilized heavily after the Revolutionary War by pioneers seeking new lands and opportunities within the newly opened Northwest Territory, which became the states of Ohio, Illinois, Indiana, Michigan, and Wisconsin.

THE JOURNEY FORWARD

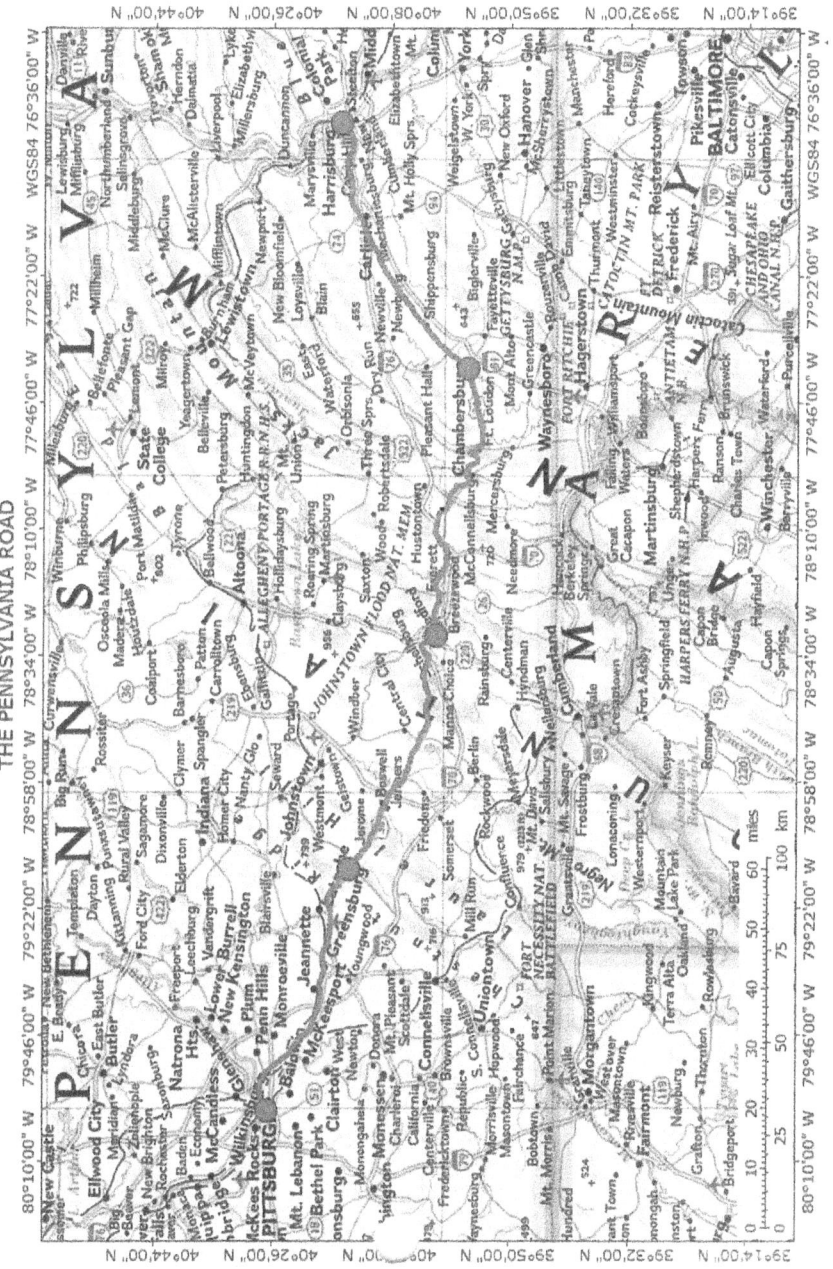

The Pennsylvania Road / Forbes Trail

THE BIG SEWICKLEY SETTLEMENT

The Big Sewickley Settlement was in Mount Pleasant Township, Westmoreland County, Pennsylvania, along the Big Sewickley Creek. It was considered the western frontier from 1783, the time right after the American Revolutionary War, until 1825.

The settlement was named for a nearby creek and bordered next to the Sewickley Manor. The Sewickley Manor was one of a series of estates once owned by the founding Penn family. Some of the richest farms in Westmoreland County were located on this manor. It also had beneath its soil a wealth of minerals.

Mount Pleasant Township was one of the eleven original townships in the newly created Westmoreland County, laid out in 1773, when the county was established. There were settlers in this area before 1770, but between 1770 and 1780 quite a settlement was made on the Big Sewickley Creek.

When the first settlers came to the township, they found it occupied by roving Native American bands with temporary villages and camps, but no permanent villages.

The first settlers were mostly young men of German descent. In the 1790s, the total taxable inhabitants were 378, but nearly twice that number were likely either renting lands or working for landowners.

After the early settlers cleared their lands and built log houses, farming was the principal occupation. The rich limestone clay soil raised good crops, chiefly grains.

In 1788, the residents of Mount Pleasant Township petitioned the court to establish a new township around the area next to the Loyalhanna

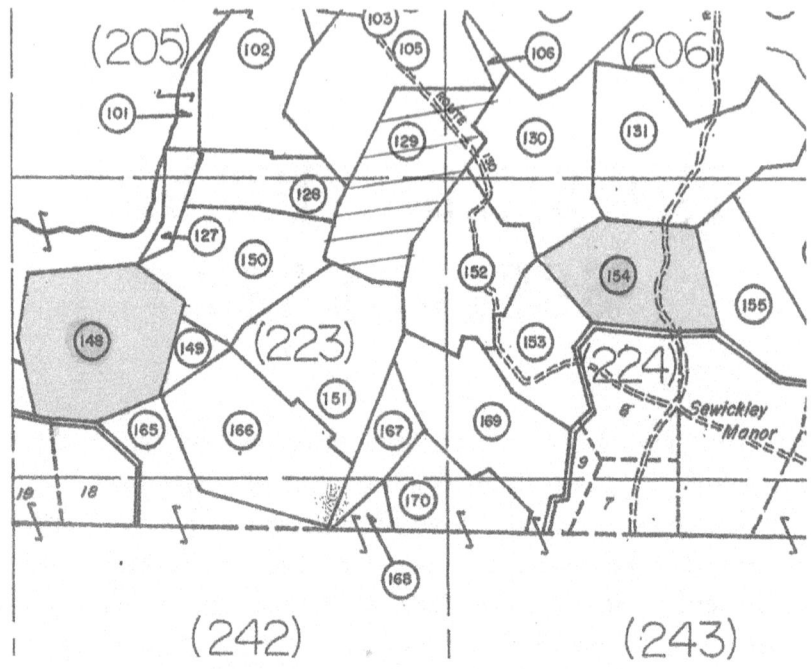

Unity Township Patantee Map, Closeup

This patentee map shows the locations of the earliest landowners of the county, in other words, those who bought their land directly from the colony or state. The prospective owner applied to the colony or state, which involved three transactions: (1) After paying a fee, the prospective landowner received a warrant authorizing the tract to be surveyed. (2) After paying a second fee, a deputy surveyor conducted a survey. (3) After paying a final fee, a patent was issued conveying final title. Many years could have separated these three transactions, and ownership might change hands multiple times between the warrant, survey, and patent. After a tract was transferred to a private individual, subsequent transactions were recorded in the county courthouse. For Robinson family properties.

Robinson Properties
- 129 Robert Jameson's property
- 148 Robert Robinson's property
- 154 John and Margaret Robinson's property

The enlarged section of the southwestern portion of the Westmoreland County map shows that John and Margaret Robinson's property is number 154. The property is next to the historical Sewickley Manor. Route 981 cuts right through the property. The property of Robert Jameson, Margaret Robinson's brother, is lot number 129. Lot number 148 marks Robert Robinson's property on the map.

Creek, based on the inconveniently large size of the existing Mount Pleasant Township, which made travel of long distances to conduct township affairs very difficult. Therefore, on September 23, 1789, Unity Township was incorporated.

+++

The Robinson, Smith, and Weir families journeyed across the state of Pennsylvania and through the mountains and, finally, in the fall of 1778 arrived and settled in the Big Sewickley Settlement. The families brought only a few necessities with them. A rifle and an ax were top items on their moving list. Other essential items included a hoe, a metal V-shaped plow, a hammer, and a saw. Other tools were made at the settlement site. Livestock generally included a horse, a cow for milk, perhaps a few sheep herded by a dog, and a pig or two. The women probably brought an iron kettle, a few pots and pans, and a spinning wheel for spinning the sheep's wool into yarn for clothing. Blankets, a family bible, and perhaps a few china plates were the only other items brought to their new home.

John Robinson had already been settled in the Big Sewickley Settlement since 1771 with his wife, Margaret, and their children. They had established a farmstead of 167 acres.

All the families stayed on the John Robinson plantation after arriving in Westmoreland County. Shortly thereafter, Robert staked out property to claim a few miles to the west of his brother John's homestead that Robert called "Salle."

Robert's home on Salle was probably a log cabin 20 to 30 feet long and 15 to 20 feet wide. He chopped down trees with his ax, and neighbors gathered to help him raise the logs to build the cabin. The women and young children filled the spaces between the logs with clay dirt, moss, or mud. Occasions when neighbors came together to help construct a cabin were called "house-raisings." House-raisings generally turned into parties called "frolics."

Since nails were not available, the boys of the family whittled wooden pegs to use for securing the cabin roof, which was made of overlapping boards. One side of the cabin included a large fireplace for cooking and warmth. The cabin had one door and sometimes one window covered

FORM No. 1.

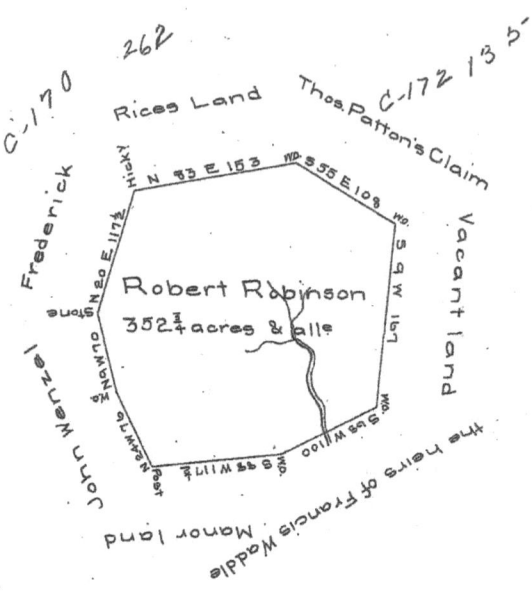

In pursuance ———— bearing date August 24th 1786 surveyed November 6th following unto Robert Robinson the above discribed tract of land situate on the waters of Sewickley ——— in Mount Pleasant township Westmoreland County Containing three hundred and fifty two acres & ¾ and allowance of six pr. cent for roads &c.

                                    Benj Lodge D.S.
To John Lukens Esq⎫
Surveyor General ⎭

IN TESTIMONY that the above is a copy of the original remaining on file in the Department of Internal Affairs of Pennsylvania, made conformably to an Act of Assembly approved the 16th day of

Robert Robinson, Mount Pleasant Property, Survey of Salle, 1786

by paper greased with animal fat. Greasing made the paper easy to see through and resistant to rain.

At first, the cabin floor was dirt, which they replaced with puncheons, large logs split lengthwise in half. They were laid flat side up on the dirt to form a floor. Likewise, tables and benches were made from split logs of varying sizes. When time permitted, most families added a loft; this was where the children slept. Besides providing room to cook and sleep, the cabin served as a workshop for making tools and whittling kitchen utensils such as bowls and forks.

The Robinson's worked from dawn to dusk to clear their land and plant a crop of corn. Seeds readily grew in the rich never-before-farmed land. With only a hoe and a plow, Robert could produce thirty to fifty bushels of corn per acre. The corn was ground into cornmeal between two heavy stones. Cornmeal was used in baking a variety of breads. They also made whiskey from corn. Peaches were the first fruit trees planted because they bore fruit within two to three years. Peach brandy was a favorite frontier drink.

The brothers hunted wild game such as turkey, duck, deer, bear, opossum, and rabbit. Wild turkeys were so fat they were easy targets as they sat in trees or walked along the ground. As livestock numbers increased, they butchered pigs and pork became a regular meat. Since there was no refrigeration, the meat was preserved by smoking, sun-drying, or salt-curing. Salt was a valuable necessity, but it was in short supply on the frontier and cost a great deal if it could be bought at all. Milk supplied by the family's cow was the chief drink. It was also churned into butter.

The women and girls planted vegetable gardens. They grew turnips, pumpkins, beans, cabbages, and potatoes. Dill and sage were the most common herbs grown. Women and children also gathered wild fruits and nuts such as berries, plums, grapes, crab apples, walnuts, and hickory nuts. Wild greens were gathered for eating and for brewing tea.

The growing Big Sewickley Settlement soon had a blacksmith, a woodcrafter, and a frontier store run by a peddler who brought basic goods from the east. Peddlers sold items such as cloth, nails, copper or iron pots, tools, lead for bullets, and gunpowder. The peddlers or storekeepers were generally paid in cornmeal, furs, or corn whiskey. They also established a mill for grinding corn and a sawmill for processing logs into planks.

Rachel Robinson and Lavina Weir were responsible for providing clothing. The first clothing of frontiersmen was made of deerskins, sewn together and decorated with fringe. The women disliked working with the animal skins; they preferred to raise a crop of flax, from which linen could be spun. Sheep were sheared each year for wool. Both flax and wool were spun into yarn on a spinning wheel. Linsey-woolsey, a combination of flax and wool, was the favorite material for making clothing. Pure linen was cooler and therefore best for summer. The men, women, and children often did not wear shoes in warm weather. The shoes they wore at other times were made from animal hides.

The families had little leisure time, but when a social occasion presented itself, they enjoyed the time immensely. House-raisings, weddings, harvest competitions, and quilting bees provided a much-needed break from work. Weddings brought guests from miles away, and celebrations often lasted two or three days. Women prepared mountains of food for feasting, corn whiskey and peach brandy flowed freely, and dancing to a fiddler's music could go on all night. Regardless of the occasion, any men who were present usually engaged in sporting matches of wrestling, shooting, and racing.

Harvest fun included corn-husking contests. Groups of people sat around roughly equal piles of recently harvested corn. When given the signal to start, each group worked quickly to try to husk their entire pile first. Drinking, dancing, and sporting events accompanied the husking parties. Quilting bees were more than women's sewing get-togethers. They included men and children. The men drank whiskey and talked of local happenings. Children ran and played among the adults. Dancing was also a favorite activity at quilting bees. This was life in the Big Sewickley Settlement in the 1780s.

+++

While William's family continued to live at the Conocoheaque Settlement, William continued to live with his brother Robert and helped on the plantations of his brothers at the Big Sewickley Settlement during this time. Lavina and Samuel Weir also lived with Robert and Rachel until they decided to move to Washington County, Pennsylvania.

On August 14, 1780, Robert's son, Robert S. Robinson, was born at the Big Sewickley Settlement, Pennsylvania.

In spring of 1781, Robert Robinson, his sister Lavina Robinson Weir, and her husband, Samuel Weir, with their children traveled to Zollarsville, Washington County, Pennsylvania to find their own place to live. They tarried awhile, but finally Lavina and Samuel settled in Pigeon Creek near the present-day town of Vanceville, Washington County, Pennsylvania.

In the fall of 1781, in order to make some money while in Washington County, Robert and Samuel were on the payroll as guards to the commissioners to run a temporary line between the states of Pennsylvania and Virginia from September 28 to October 5, 1781. This opportunity to make some money was because the boundaries between the colonies were not clearly defined. Much of the western frontier was not surveyed because it was Indian land and considered to be dangerous. During this period, Pennsylvania's colonial government was embroiled in long-standing disputes with Virginia and other states. Virginia claimed that western Pennsylvania was part of its colony and called it West Augusta District. The official boundaries were not established until 1784–1785.

+++

Sometime in 1782, tragedy struck the family when John, the family trailblazer, died after falling from a horse in Mount Pleasant Township, Westmoreland County, Pennsylvania. John and Margaret Jameson Robinson had been married for fifteen years when he died. The Robinson and Jameson families supported John's wife and children in various ways so that Margaret and the children could remain living on their plantation.

As part of their patriotic service, in 1783, Robert and William Robinson paid taxes in Mount Pleasant Township, Westmoreland County, Pennsylvania. Robert was taxed on 150 acres with three horses, four cattle, and one sheep. William was taxed on one horse. John's widowed wife, Margaret Robinson paid taxes on 100 acres of land and one horse, two cattle, and four sheep. Payment of the 1783 taxes was considered a patriotic act to help the country reduce its debt from the Revolutionary War.[1]

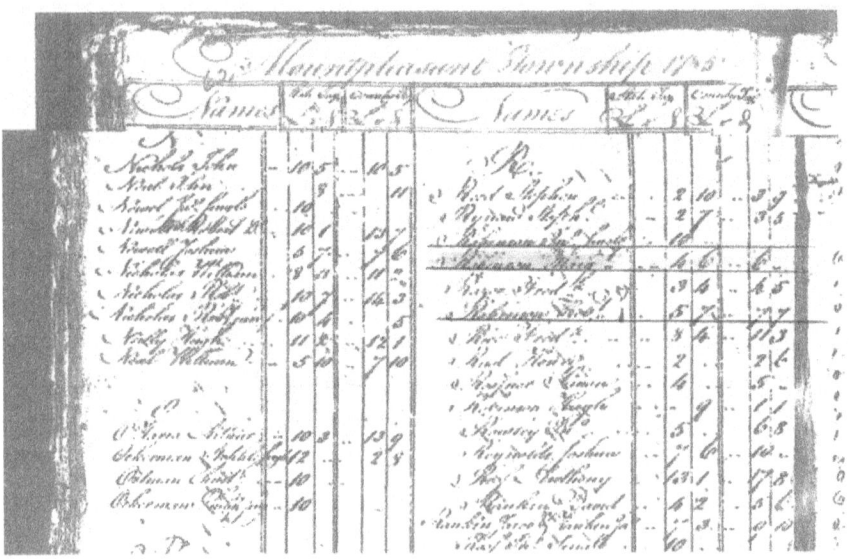

Mountpleasant Township 1783 Tax Document

Mountpleasant Township 1785 Tax Document
The documents above for the Mount Pleasant Township tax roll show the names of Margaret Robinson, Robert Robinson, and William Robinson as having paid taxes.

THEIR STORIES

THESE ARE THE INDIVIDUAL STORIES OF THE ROBINSONS who immigrated to British America, fought in the War of Independence, and settled the frontier of the new American lands. This section tells what is known of the lives of the first Robinson immigrants, their children, and their grandchildren in the new world, dating from 1770 to the mid-1800s.

Robert Robinson Sr. Family

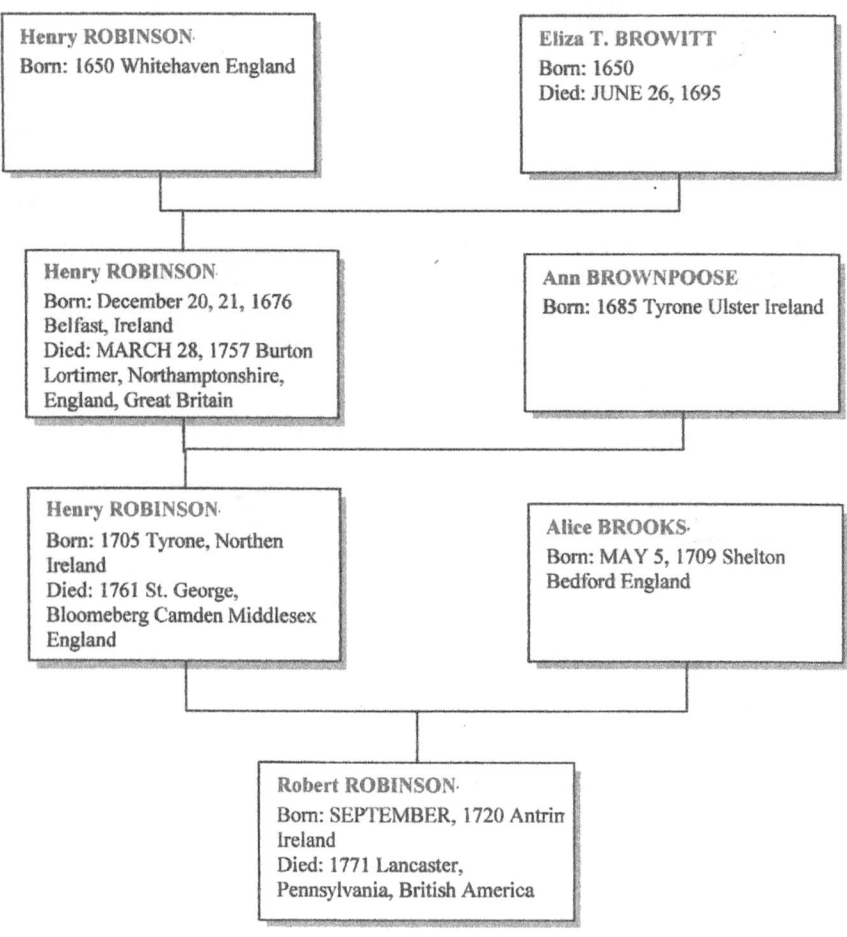

Robert Robinson Sr. Ancestry Chart
The known ancestry of the Robinson family dates back to 1650 in Whitehaven, England.

ROBERT SR. & ISABELLA

Robert Robinson Sr. was born in September 1720 in Antrim County, Ireland. He was married to Isabella Harris Robinson, who was born in 1721 in Ireland. They had five children:

William, born 1735;
Robert Jr., born 1739;
John, twin to Jennie, born 1740;
Jennie (Jane), twin to John, born 1740; and
Lavina (Levey), born in 1745.

In the year 1770, Robert and Isabella, at the ages of fifty and fifty-one years old, respectively, decided to leave Ireland with their daughter Jennie and sail to British America to live with their other children who had already settled in the new land. Robert Sr. would leave behind an ancestor lineage that dates to the year 1650 (see *family chart, p. 42*).

Most of the family had already left Ireland by the time Robert Sr. Isabella, and Jennie followed the rest of the family to British America just a year after son John started the family's journey. They arrived in Philadelphia on October 25, 1771, on the brig named *Polly*.

Finding a passenger list or other documentation of their voyage is difficult to impossible as it is likely that their arrival was not recorded. The Robinsons were British subjects and not required to sign an oath of allegiance upon arrival in Philadelphia, so documentation may be nonexistent.

Their son William traveled to the port to gather his parents and sister and take them to the family homestead. Unfortunately, while on the journey from Philadelphia to the family homestead in Marietta, Pennsylvania, the original Irish matriarch, Isabella, died suddenly in Derry, Dauphin County, Pennsylvania, British America.

They had already traveled approximately ninety-five miles from Philadelphia and had only sixteen miles remaining to get to the family homestead in Marietta. She would be buried at the Derry Church. The Derry Churchyard Cemetery is the oldest pioneer graveyard in Dauphin County.

In late 1771, not long after his wife's death, the Irish immigrant and family's patriarch, Robert Sr., died at the family homestead in Marietta, Lancaster County, Pennsylvania, British America. He is buried in Lancaster.

It was now up to Robert and Isabella's children, the next generation, to continue the journey.

WILLIAM & JANE

William Robinson, born in 1735, was the oldest son of Robert and Isabella Harris Robinson. His father and mother were fifteen years old and fourteen years old, respectively, at the time of his birth.

He emigrated from Maghera, Londonderry County, Ireland, and arrived at the port of Philadelphia, Pennsylvania, British America, on June 21, 1770, via Dublin on the brig named *Connolly* with his young son named William Jr.

Upon arriving, William waited in Philadelphia until the arrival of his brother Robert in July.

Unfortunately, William Jr. died twenty-one days after their arrival, and he was buried at the Saint Michaelis and Zion Cemetery in Philadelphia. He apparently caught a fever, possibly smallpox or yellow fever, during the journey on the ship.

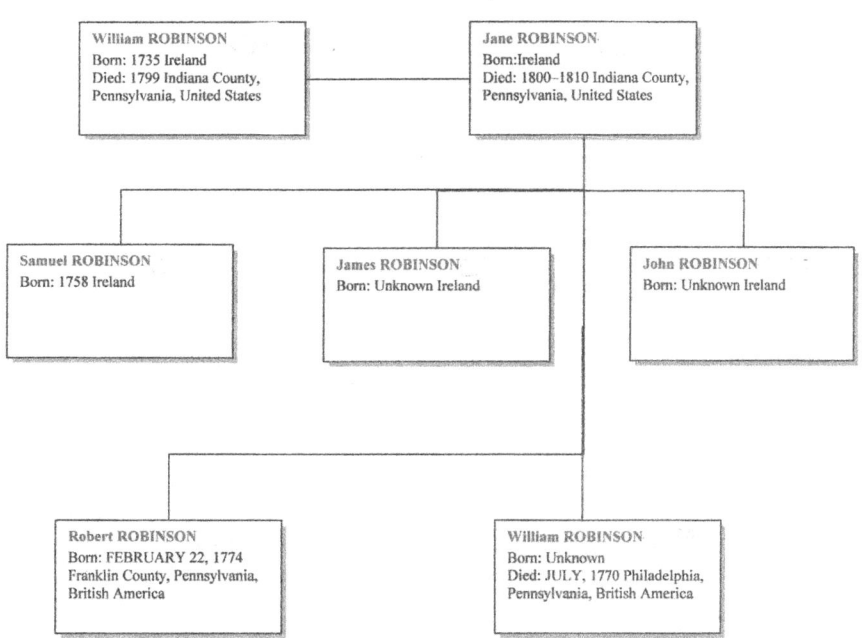

William Robinson Family Chart

William stayed near his brother Robert and sister-in-law Rachel, and his sister Lavina and her family for most of the journey. William's wife and their sons remained in Ireland and would arrive in British America at various times in the coming years.

In 1771, William purchased his plantation of 150 acres of land in Lancaster County. He had two horses and five cattle.[1]

In 1772, the Lancaster County Proprietary and State Tax list shows that William paid taxes of nine pounds for 100 acres and two horses and three cattle. He had sold 50 acres and two cattle between 1771 and 1772. He sold the land and cattle to pay for his return trip to Ireland in early 1773 to make arrangements to bring his family to British America in 1774.

In 1773, the Lancaster County Proprietary and State Tax list shows that William paid taxes of nine pounds for 100 acres and two horses and four cattle.

Meanwhile, in early 1773, William returned to Ireland to prepare to bring his family to British America. William and Jane had five children: William, Samuel, James, John, and Robert. According to their plan, William Robinson's family would get transportation to British America either as a petty criminal, indentured servant, or apprentice. To get passage back to British America in the summer of 1773, William was arrested and sentenced to transportation at a "Sessions of Gaol Delivery" ("gaol" means jail).

Of worthwhile note, of the convicts dispatched to the Americas in colonial times, all but a relatively insignificant minority belonged to the poorest class; of these, most were sentenced for crimes that today might incur a small fine or, more likely, probation. Roughly half were sentenced by the courts in and around London.

It was a clever way to get free passage to British America; other members of William Robinson's family utilized this method of transportation also, including his wife, Jane. She arrived in Philadelphia in January 1774 as a convict of a petty crime. She was sentenced in London to transportation at the "Sessions of Gaol Delivery."

Jane was pregnant during the journey and would give birth to another son they named Robert, soon after arriving in British America.

Even after William and Jane's sons arrived in America, they would not be able to join the family until their servitude and apprenticeship terms were completed. It was common for boys to learn a trade as an apprentice, and parents often arranged apprenticeships for their children. The contracts usually lasted several years. The contract required the "master" to provide the apprentice with professional training, some schooling, food, clothing, and moral supervision in the absence of a parent. After completing the apprenticeship, the young man became a "journeyman." The "master" would pay the journeyman "freedom dues," like new clothing and a set of tools, to start their career.

William and Jane's son Samuel arrived in Philadelphia in January 1774 as an indentured servant. James arrived on March 6, 1772, but would be an apprentice until July 1774. John arrived March 1, 1773, and would be an indentured servant as an apprentice until 1777.

After William's return to British America, he would purchase, on December 13, 1773, 200 acres of land in Westmoreland County, Pennsylvania. He would pay the state of Pennsylvania ten pounds for the 200 acres. This purchase evidently turned into 350 acres of land as shown on the land survey. As the survey dated June 11, 1773, shows, there is nothing around the surveyed land and the only way to get to it was a trading path *(see land survey, p. 49)*. There were very few inhabitants in this territory at the time.

William and Jane had five children:

William Robinson Jr.

Birth date and age unknown, William Jr. died shortly after arriving in Philadelphia, Pennsylvania, British America. The date of death is listed as July 11, 1770, in Philadelphia, Pennsylvania, British America, and he was buried at the Saint Michaelis and Zion Cemetery in Philadelphia on the same date.

Infant William Robinson, date of death, July 11, 1779

Samuel Robinson

Samuel was born in 1758 in Ireland. He departed from London sometime around January 2–9, 1774, and arrived in Philadelphia, Pennsylvania, British America, on a ship named *Amelia*, as an indentured servant. He was listed on the *Amelia* passenger list as a brick maker and was sixteen years old at the time. He may have been an indentured servant to his father, since there is no time of servitude or assigned name referenced on any of the ship's documents.

James Robinson

Birth date unknown, James departed from London on March 6, 1772, and arrived in Philadelphia as an apprentice. He was an indentured servant to Seth Mattack, and he was assigned for two years and four months. He was also given one quarter's night schooling in the cooper's trade (barrel making) and served his apprenticeship in Philadelphia.* He would have been a free man in July 1774.

John Robinson

Birth date unknown, John arrived in Philadelphia on March 1, 1773, as an indentured servant to Joseph Moore and his assigns. He was listed as an apprentice on the passenger documents and was taught the cordwainers trade (shoemaker) for the next four years and eight months.

Robert Robinson

Robert was born February 22, 1774, at the Conococheague Settlement in Franklin County, Pennsylvania. He was born nine months after his father, William, returned to Ireland to see his family and a little over a month after his mother, Jane, arrived in British America.

---

*The term "one quarter's" refers to a season of the year and time of day when the person is least needed for farming duties. The time period is approximately three months.

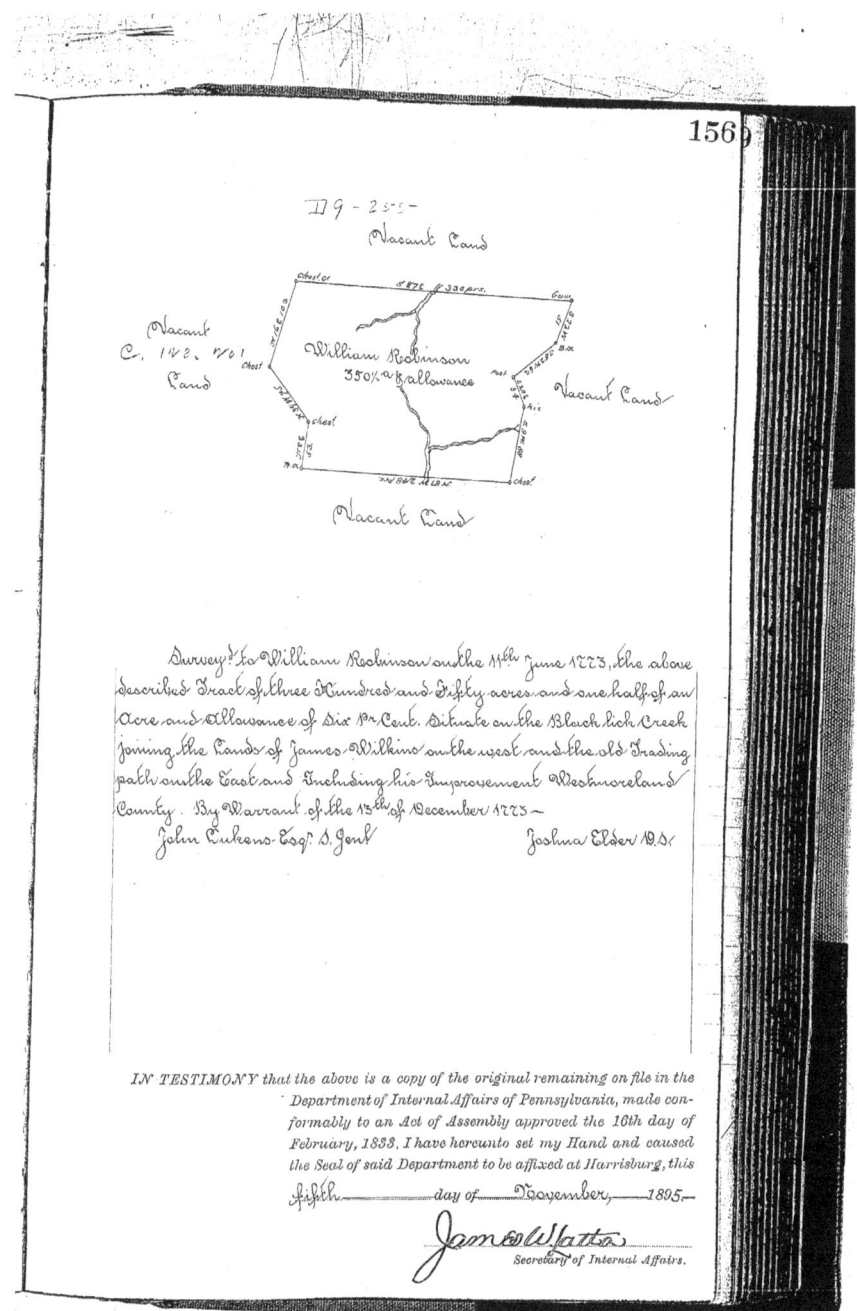

William Robinson, 1773 Land Warrant

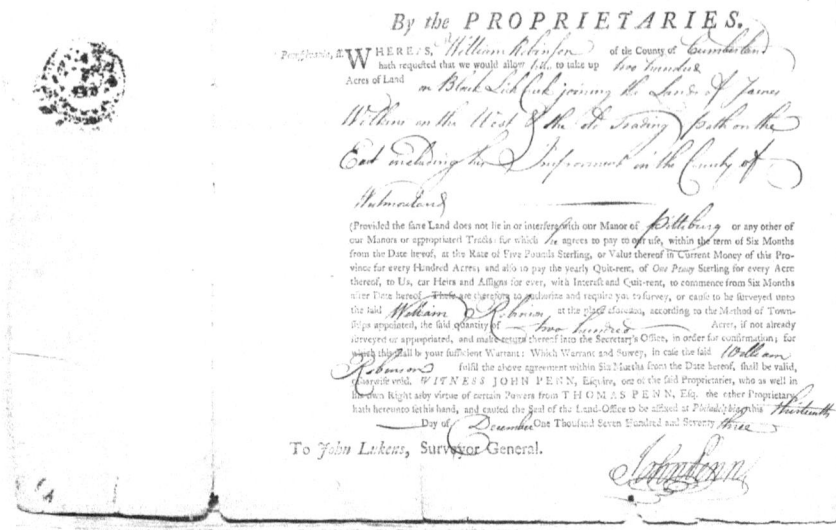

William Robinson, 1773 Land Warrant

Jane did not join William on the western frontier until sometime in 1788–1789. Their sons remained in Cumberland County, Pennsylvania. In the 1790 Census for Armstrong Township *(see 1790 Census, below)* in Westmoreland County, Pennsylvania, the first column shows "Free White Males 16+" the second column shows "Free White Males under 16" and the third column shows "Free White Females." William would have been fifty-five years old, at the time of the 1790 Census.

William and Jane continued to live on the frontier for the next ten years. In 1798, William paid taxes on 150 acres of land in Armstrong Township, Westmoreland County. He had one house worth eight dollars, and 150 acres worth three hundred dollars.

1790 Census

THE JOURNEY FORWARD

1798 Tax Document

Unfortunately, in early December 1799, William Robinson passed away at his plantation at the age of sixty-four. William's Last Testament and Will was dated January 21, 1797.[2] His health must have been on the decline since in his will, he states of "being of sick body but of good and perfect memory." The following are the highlights of the will:

1. His sons Samuel, James, and John received real estate as divided and laid off to them.
2. His wife, Jane, received a young bay mare and her saddle, two cows, three sheep, the household furniture, and the privilege of what she would need for the use of the orchard and garden.
3. His son Robert was willed that part of real estate that William lived on, and the remaining part of the stock and all farming equipment. Also, Robert was given a colt.
4. While Jane lived, Robert was to provide a yearly allowance of twelve bushels of wheat and 100 weight of meat beef for her support.
5. John Robinson Sr. (Capt. John) and James Smith Esq. (Jennie Robinson Smith's son) were appointed as executors of his will.

Since all his sons were over the age of twenty-one years, the transfer of William's estate was rather quick, about six weeks. The official recording of the estate transfer was dated February 6, 1802. The following document shows the recording of the transfer of the original 200 acres that William purchased from the state of Pennsylvania to his sons.

William's Last Will and Testament, 1797
The will was witnessed by Robert Little and Alexander Templeton and proven by the Orphans Court and recorded on December 26, 1799. The Abstract of Wills showed that it was proven on December 26, 1799.

William Robinson, Land Transfer

William's son Robert continued to live on the plantation for several years. The 1800 Census of Armstrong Township shows that Robert was living there with three males under 10 years of age and one male 26–44 years old. (He would have been twenty-six years old at the time.) The census showed that there was one female under 10 years of age, one female 10–25 years of age (probably his wife), one female 45+ years of age (probably his mother, Jane), and one slave (probably an indentured servant).

1800 Census of Armstrong Township

Then ten years later, the 1810 Census of Armstrong Township, shows that William's youngest son, Robert, had at his plantation two males under 10 years of age, two males 10–15 years of age, one male 26–44 years of age (himself), three females under 10 years of age, one female 10–15 years of age, and one female 26–44 years of age (probably his wife).

This means that Jane Robinson, William's wife, died sometime between the 1800 Census and the 1810 Census. With the deaths of Jane and William, this marks the end of the second generation in America for their family. Their son, Robert and his family continued to live on the western frontier amongst his cousins and his namesake, his uncle Robert.

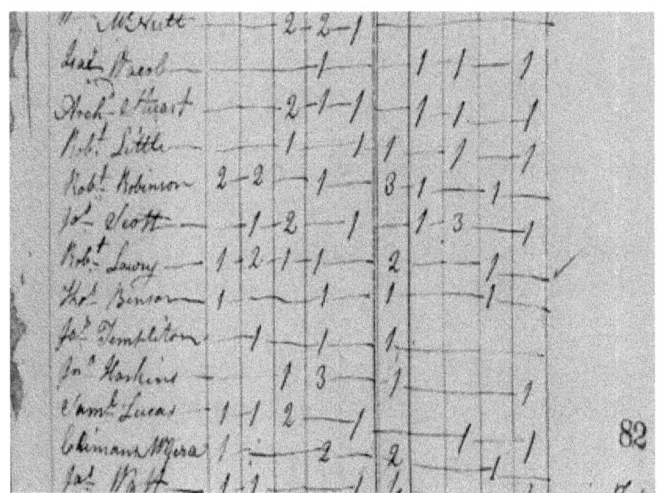

1810 Census of Armstrong Township

ROBERT JR. & RACHEL

Robert Robinson Jr., born in 1739, was the second son of Robert and Isabella Harris Robinson. His father and mother were nineteen years old and eighteen years old, respectively, at the time of his birth.

Before their journey to British America, Robert married Rachel Weir (older sister of brother-in-law Samuel Weir) in November 1769. Rachel was pregnant with their first child during the ocean voyage.

Robert was a very hardworking man and was always willing to work any way possible to make money, as this story will show. He eventually became the leader of this family once they arrived in British America, and he believed that a better life was available in the new country.

Robert Robinson Family

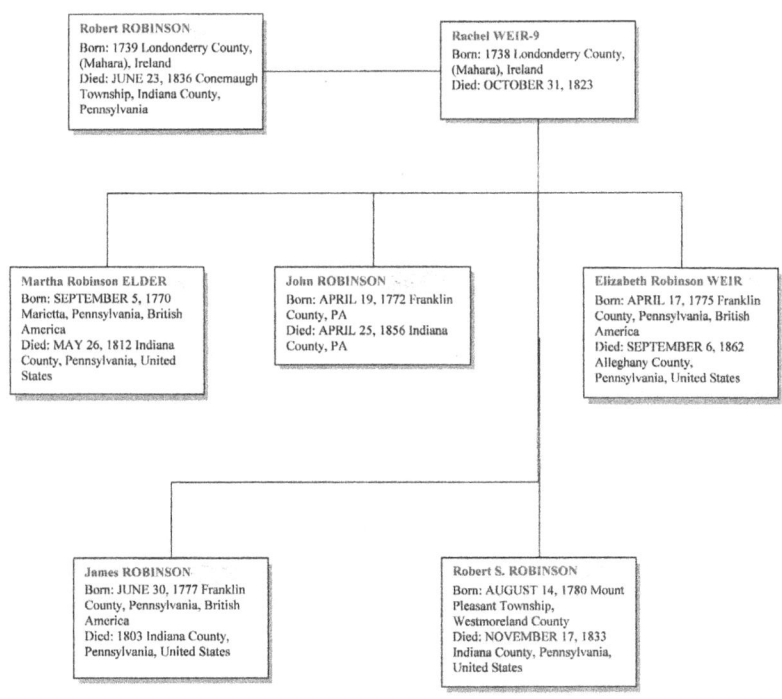

Robert Robinson Family Chart

Like most families emigrating to British America at the time, the family members stayed together. Throughout this journey, Robert stayed close with his older brother, William, and his youngest sister, Lavina, and her husband, Samuel Weir, and their family.

During their time in Lancaster County, several children were born into the family. Robert and Rachel's children were Martha, John, Elizabeth, James, and Robert S.

Martha Robinson Elder

Martha was born in Marietta, Lancaster County, Pennsylvania, on September 5, 1770. At the age of twenty-two, she would marry James Elder of Elders Ridge on December 25, 1792, in Westmoreland County, Pennsylvania.

James Elder was the oldest son of Robert Elder, and James and Martha settled on the half of the farm that contained the first buildings that were built. He was a large muscular man, full of courage and capable of great endurance and thus was well fitted for pioneer life.[1]

During the American Revolutionary War, James served as an Ensign with the 2nd Battalion, 2nd Company of the Westmoreland County Militia, under the command of James Sloan.[2]

The children of James and Martha Elder were Robert R., born October 8, 1793; David, born August 22, 1796; John, born October 2, 1797; Polly, born October 22, 1799; Joshua, born January 18, 1802; James, born February 18, 1804; Rachel, born December 18, 1806; and Thomas, born March 1, 1810.

Martha died on May 26, 1812, at forty-two years of age. Martha's husband, James Elder, died April 13, 1813, his birthday. Both are buried at the Ebenezer graveyard in Saltsburg, Pennsylvania.

Martha Elder, Headstone

Martha and James Elder, Headstones

Captain John Robinson

John (later to be known as Captain John) was born in Cumberland County (now Franklin County), Pennsylvania, on April 19, 1772. On December 6, 1798, he married Mary Weir of Washington County, Pennsylvania. However, she died on Tuesday, March 13, 1804, in her thirtieth year and was buried in the Robinson River Hill graveyard on the original family land called "York."

John was a hardworking and ambitious man. He purchased his first piece of land on September 25, 1788, at the age of sixteen years. He would continue to add to this acreage during his lifetime so that he had over several hundred acres at the time of his death.

John and Mary Robinson had three sons: Robert W., born September 25, 1799; Adam, born April 15, 1801; and James W. Robinson, born February 21, 1803.

In 1805, John Robinson was elected captain of a volunteer militia company, which drilled near Indiana.* He would parade his men to Indiana, Pennsylvania, about twenty miles from his home. His regimentals were blue coat with cuffs, collars, and long skirt (kilt) faced with red. The picture on shows the regimental coat *(see image, p. 59)*.

On May 30, 1805, John Robinson married Jane Scott Marshall of Indiana County, Pennsylvania. They purchased and lived on a farm called the "Iconium," whose lands were situated about a mile north of the original York lands of his father.

The nine children of John and Jane Scott were Jennie, born October 30, 1806, who died as an infant on March 24, 1808, and is buried at Robinson River Hill cemetery; John M., born December 11, 1808; Rachel, born October 8, 1810; Jane, born August 25, 1812; William M., born July 14, 1814; Samuel S., born August 5, 1816; Thomas W., born December 11, 1818; Eliza, born January 17, 1821; and Mariah, born January 29, 1826.

---

*Volunteer militia units were recognized by the Act of March 21, 1803, and exempted from the regular compulsory militia. One early volunteer unit came into existence about 1805 in Indiana County, Pennsylvania.

Capt. John's Regimental Coat

In 1806, John became one of the first ruling elders at the Ebenezer Presbyterian Church and later became one of the first elders at Saltsburg Presbyterian Church on August 1, 1824.

Sometime about October 1841, John was thrown from his horse and his hip joint was injured so that he was ever Lid aside from active work. But how many can tell of the wonderful influence for good as he sat so seriously in his chimney corner. That influence for Christ and the welfare of souls was felt further, possibly than if no such affliction had befallen him.[3]

Capt. John Robinson, Gravestone, 1856; "Aged 84" Years

Jane S. Robinson, Gravestone; "Aged 79 Years"

John died on April 25, 1856, at the age of eighty-four. His wife, Jane Scott, died on November 10, 1860, at the age of seventy-nine. The remains of both were taken from the Robinson River Hill Cemetery to Edgewood Cemetery in Saltsburg, Pennsylvania.

Elizabeth Robinson Weir

Elizabeth "Betsy" Robinson was born in Cumberland County (now Franklin County), Pennsylvania, on April 17, 1775. She was married to her cousin Thomas Weir, born in 1765 in Ireland, of Washington County, Pennsylvania. Thomas Weir is the first son of Lavina (the youngest sister of Robert) and Samuel Weir.

Betsy died in Allegheny County, Pennsylvania, on September 6, 1862, at eighty-seven years old and is buried at Round Hill Church near Pittsburgh, Pennsylvania. Thomas died in December 1848 and was buried at his own request on his farm near the mouth of Pigeon Creek in Washington County, Pennsylvania.

They had three sons and three daughters: Rachel, Jane, Adam, Robert, William, and Martha.

James Robinson

James Robinson was born in Cumberland County (now Franklin County) on June 30, 1777. He was married to Mary Laughlin near Indiana, Pennsylvania. They lived at the home of his parents, Robert and Rachel Robinson, on the York lands.

Mary died suddenly in 1803, and James died sometime in November or early December 1807 at the age of thirty. In his will, probated on December 14, 1807, James bequeathed two volumes of Scotts family bibles to his brother John, a great coat to his brother Robert S., and his rifle to his father. His namesake, James W., son of his brother John, received a watch. Three hundred acres of land were divided among his brothers and father.

Both James and Mary are buried at the Robinson River Hill Cemetery on the original land known as York and left no direct descendants.

Robert S. Robinson, Headstone, 1833, "Aged 53 Yrs."

Robert S. Robinson

Robert S. Robinson was born at the Big Sewickley Settlement in Mount Pleasant Township, Pennsylvania, on August 14, 1780. He was married to Elizabeth Black on June 5, 1806. They lived on a farm just north of the original York homestead. This house is in the valley north of where Nowrytown is now located.

He died November 17, 1833, at age fifty-three from yellow fever. He caught the fever from his daughter Jane, who died one-and-a-half months earlier on September 30, 1833, at the age of thirteen years.

Shortly after his death, his widow, Elizabeth, moved to Saltsburg, Pennsylvania, where she lived until the time of her death on January 10, 1874, at the age of eighty-nine. Both were buried at the Edgewood Cemetery in Saltsburg, Pennsylvania.

Their children were James B., born April 7, 1807; Robert; born March 26, 1810; John H., born April 21, 1812; Thomas W., born February 24, 1814; Johnston Stearns, born April 22, 1816; William Clark, born August 26, 1818; Jane B., born October 9, 1820; David Elder Robinson, born December 20, 1823; and Elizabeth W., born July 22, 1826.

In Robert's will dated November 8, 1833, the "freehold estate" was bequeathed to his son Robert.** His wife, Elizabeth, was bequeathed one-third of the personal property. The other two-thirds of the personal property was divided between his sons Robert and John. His sons James B., Thomas W., and Johnston S. were given ten dollars each. His sons William Clark and David Elder were given ten dollars each when they reached twenty-one years old. His daughter Elizabeth was given twenty dollars at the age of twenty-one years. In his will, he directed that his son John was to provide six months of schooling for William Clark, and for William Clark to be taught a trade. Additionally, Elizabeth and David E. were to be provided schooling at the age of fifteen years, and for David E. to be taught a trade.

** A freehold estate is an estate in which you have exclusive rights to enjoy the possession of a property for an undefined length of time.

As part of his legacy, he was one of the first grand jurors on the first grand jury convened in December 1806. In 1809, 1810, and 1811, Robert S. Robinson was a commissioner in Conemaugh Township. From 1812 to 1815, he was the sheriff of Conemaugh Township.

JOHN & MARGARET

John Robinson was the third born of Robert Sr. and Isabella Robinson, but the first of the Robinsons to arrive in the new colony of British America.

John was born on August 28, 1740, and was the twin brother to Jennie (Jane) Robinson. His father and mother were twenty-one years old and twenty years old, respectively, at the time of his birth. He emigrated from Maghera, Londonderry County, Ireland.

John Robinson Family

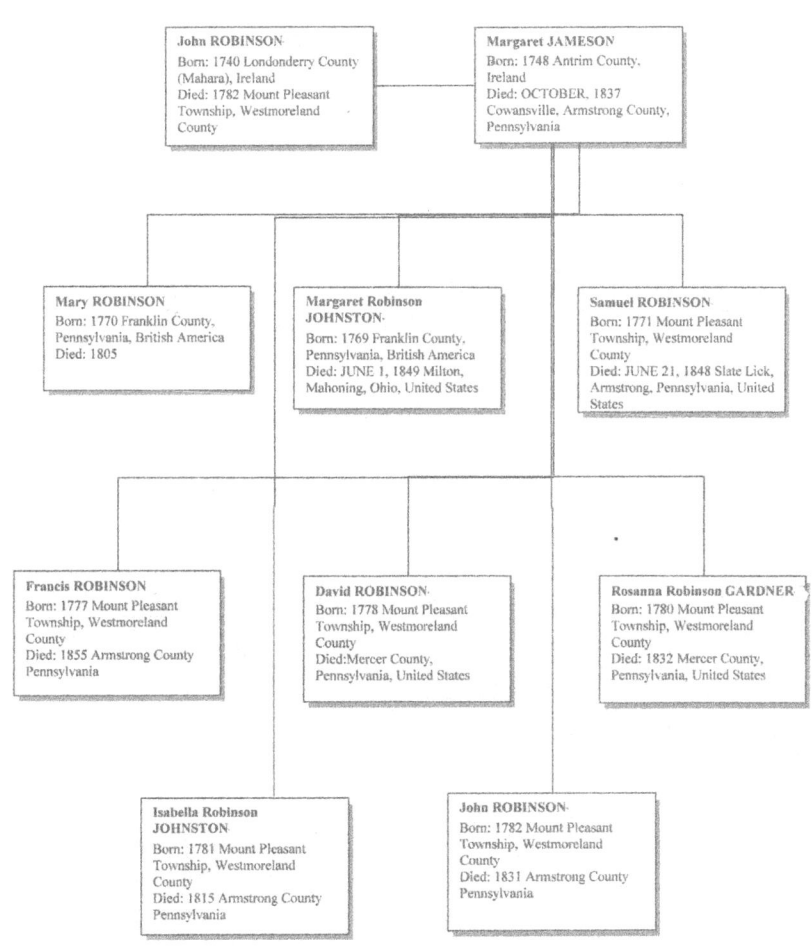

John Robinson Family Chart

His wife, Margaret, was born in 1748 in Buckna Church Parish, Broughshane, Antrim County, Ireland. Margaret's father, Francis Jameson, was twenty-eight years old, and her mother, Margaret Jameson, was twenty-eight years old at the time of her birth.

John Robinson and Margaret Jameson were married in 1766 in British America, and they had eight children together, as follows:

Margaret Robinson Johnston

Margaret was born in 1769 in Cumberland County, Pennsylvania, and died June 1, 1849, at eighty years old in Milton, Mahoning County, Ohio. She was the wife of John Johnston and the mother of Francis Robinson Johnston, who wrote the 1898 letter that confirmed her parents were married in British America in 1766.[1]

Mary Robinson

Mary was born in 1770 in Cumberland County, Pennsylvania, and died in 1805 at thirty-five years of age. Mary is mentioned in the 1793 deed of her parent's plantation, but her name is missing from the 1805 final settlement documents. Mary and Margaret were "Irish twins." This means that the two children were born to the same mother within twelve months.

Samuel Robinson

Samuel was born in early 1771 at the Sewickley Settlement in Mount Pleasant Township, Westmoreland County, Pennsylvania, and died on June 21, 1848, at seventy-seven years of age in Slate Lick, Armstrong County, Pennsylvania. He was married in 1813 to Nancy Jack Sloan, who was born in 1780 and died in 1857. Samuel Robinson is reported to have been a farmer in Armstrong County.[2]

The death dates of Samuel Robinson and his wife, Nancy Jack Sloan Robinson, are listed in the Register of Deaths, Slate Lick Presbyterian Church, Slate Lick, Armstrong County, Pennsylvania.[3] The grave stones at the Old Slate Lick Cemetery, Armstrong County, Pennsylvania, say: "Samuel Robinson, died June 21, 1848, in the 77th year of his age" and "Nancy Robinson, died March 30, 1857, in the 77th year of her age."

Francis Robinson

Francis was born in 1777 at the Big Sewickley Settlement in Mount Pleasant Township, Westmoreland County, Pennsylvania. His residence in 1850 was in Armstrong County, Pennsylvania. He died in 1855 at the age of seventy-eight.

David Robinson

David was born in 1778 at the Big Sewickley Settlement in Mount Pleasant Township, Westmoreland County, Pennsylvania. David Robinson was appointed executor of the estate of David Gardner and Rosana Robinson (his sister) in Mercer County, Pennsylvania, in 1832. Also, David Robinson is listed as a resident of Mercer County and mentioned in the estate notes of his uncle Marmaduke Jameson, brother of his mother.

Rosanna Robinson Gardner

Rosanna was born in 1780 at the Big Sewickley Settlement in Mount Pleasant Township, Westmoreland County, Pennsylvania. She married David Gardner. She died in 1832 at fifty-two years of age.

Isabella Robinson Johnston

Isabella was born in 1781 at the Big Sewickley Settlement in Mount Pleasant Township, Westmoreland County, Pennsylvania. She was the first wife of David Johnston (1779–1838). David Johnston was the brother of John Johnston, Margaret Robinson's husband. She died in 1815 in Armstrong County at thirty-four years of age.

John Robinson Jr.

John was born in 1782 at the Big Sewickley Settlement in Mount Pleasant Township, Westmoreland County, Pennsylvania. He died in 1831 at forty-nine years of age in Armstrong County.

+++

On his initial voyage to British America, John had to get creative to get passage and according to documents of bonded passengers, John was pardoned for a minor crime and sentenced to transportation to British America in December 1765. He was transported on the HMS *Tryall* in January 1766 and arrived in British America about February/March 1766 *(see image, below)*. The court documents stated he was leaving "for life."

A little over a year after his arrival, John purchased a plantation with 129 acres of land in Hopewell Township, Cumberland County, Pennsylvania, on which to reside. The warrant for the land was dated May 6, 1767, and it was surveyed on May 18, 1767.

In early 1769, John and Margaret's first child was born, a daughter named Margaret.

On April 3, 1769, the Penn family Land Office began to sell off southwestern Pennsylvania land purchased from the Six Nations at the

The HMS *Tryall* that John Robinson sailed on to British America.
The HMS *Tryall* was a 10-gun two-masted Hind class sloop of the Royal Navy launched on July 17, 1744. She was broken up on January 3, 1776, after more than twenty-eight years of service,

Council of Fort Stanwix. Immediately, settlers could legally purchase frontier land from the Land Office. At the time, this western region was part of Cumberland County. In January 1773, Westmoreland County was formed out of Cumberland County's western territory.

After the Land Office opened in the western region, John Robinson and Margaret's brothers John and Robert Jameson went to Westmoreland County to claim land and settle. Both John Robinson and Robert Jameson claimed land near the present-day town called Pleasant Unity (*see map, p. 34*). To claim a piece of land, they had to submit a letter with a detailed description, usually based on a tomahawk survey.* Once their claim became official, they proceeded to build cabins on the claimed lands.

They then returned to Franklin County for the winter. In the spring of 1770, the Jameson brothers returned with one of Margaret's sisters to keep house for them. John Robinson did not return with her brothers because he was escorting his family from Ireland in the spring and summer of 1770. Then in spring of 1771, John and Margaret and their family moved west and settled at what would be known as the Big Sewickley Settlement in Westmoreland County, Pennsylvania, where they would spend the rest of their lives.[4]

There is documentation that confirms that John Robinson already had his tract of land in Mount Pleasant Township, Westmoreland County, Pennsylvania, in 1776, as shown by the following transaction listed in Deed Book A, which states:[5]

> **I, William Mounts of Mount Pleasant Twp. in Westmoreland, for 150 lbs., have sold to Robert Taylor in County of York, an improvement, plantation, & tract of land in Mount Pleasant Twp, Westmoreland, bounded by Eagers, JOHN Robinson, containing about 340 acres. The land is situated in Sewickley Manner. Signed May 22, 1776 – Wm Mount. Wit – W. Lochry (JP), John Taylog. Recorded Sep 2, 1780.**

---

*A tomahawk survey was what a professional surveyor called a "relative" survey, which laid out a parcel of land relative to a specific point. After the settlements became more established, an actual survey could be completed.

John and Margaret continued to live on the western frontier and were joined by the rest of the Robinson family in 1778. Unfortunately, sometime in late 1782, John Robinson died from a fall off a horse in Mount Pleasant Township, Westmoreland County, Pennsylvania. John and Margaret Jameson Robinson had been married for fifteen years when he died.

Soon after, Robert was named the trustee of his brother's property and guardian of his minor children. Under the law at the time, the Orphans Court administered the estate of minors and incapacitated persons. If the father passed away, the court would appoint a guardian to manage the estate even if the mother was still living. The guardian would be responsible for the estate until the minor children became of age to inherit the estate. The legal process for guardianship took years to be settled in the courts.

The Westmoreland County Orphans Court XOC states:[6]

JOHN ROBINSON, DEC. Isabella Robinson, daughter of John Robinson Dec., being about the age of fourteen years, comes into court and chooses Robert Robinson of Unity Township to be the guardian over her person and estate until the she attains the age of twenty-one years, and the court appoints the said Robert Robinson guardian over the person and Estate of John Robinson a minor son under the age of fourteen years of the said deceased during his minority.

Robert would remain the guardian until the oldest son, Samuel, turned twenty-one years old in 1793. Until that time, Robert and William oversaw the property and were the mentors of John's sons. The estate issues resulting from John's death would linger for several years and would greatly impact the lives of Robert, William, Margaret, and Margaret's children.

One of the biggest estate problems that needed to be overcome was the ownership of "Margareta."

While probating the estate and trying to put it into a trust, Robert found that the biggest problem was ownership of John and Margaret's estate known as "Margareta." It was discovered that there was no application for a patent prior to the 1786 warrant document. Apparently, John did not previously apply for a warrant for this tract of land. Margaret then had to complete all the legal steps of the land acquisition process after John's death in order to put the land in trust for John Robinson's heirs.

First title to land in Pennsylvania was acquired through the following five-step process:
1. Application – request for land by an individual;
2. Warrant – order to survey the tract of land;
3. Survey – land measured, marked, and sketched with boundaries and an exact determination of the true acreage;
4. Return of Survey – internal document sent from the Surveyor General to the Secretary of the Land Office; and
5. Patent – final deed from the Penn family or the Commonwealth passing ownership of the tract of land to a private owner.

Because Margaret was named in every step of this process, including the first step of the application, and therefore confirms that her deceased husband had not made a prior application on the same tract of land himself after claiming it. It would take several years to correct.

Margaret continued to live on their plantation with the help of her children and John's brothers, Robert and William, as well as her brothers, until 1794.

The year after John Robinson died, the 1783 Mount Pleasant Township tax records showed that Margaret Robinson paid taxes on 100 acres of land and one horse, two cattle, and four sheep. The tax roll of Mount Pleasant Township for 1785 also shows that Margaret continued to live and pay taxes on the plantation.

This process would prove to be time-consuming and costly. In order to receive a warrant, Margaret needed to pay the state of Pennsylvania twenty pounds in gold, silver, or paper money, plus interest owed, from May 1, 1776 (ten years). The warrant was finally granted on March 28, 1786. The patent would be signed on September 7, 1790.

In 1786, approximately four years after John's death, the estate of John Robinson was placed in a trust, with the granting of the warrant when Samuel reached the age of twenty-one years old, which would be in 1793. Robert Robinson would be faced with another similar situation several years later with the estate of his son James.

Margaret Robinson owned 167 acres as per the warrant dated March

28, 1786. The land had to be put into a trust since at that time a widow could not own land. The survey of the property was done on June 18, 1788. These are the official records associated with the deed for the property. The warrant for land in Mount. Pleasant Township, Westmoreland County, for Margaret Robinson in trust for herself and the heirs of John Robinson, deceased, is dated March 1786. The neighbors are listed as Joseph Eagon's heirs: Robert Nichols, John Peoples, Samuel Serrils, and Robert Telor. *(See documents, pp. 73, 74, 77, 78, 79, and 80.)*

On the 1786 Pennsylvania State and County Tax and Exoneration List, John Robinson is listed as the freeman of bondsman Robert Jameson. This means that Robert Jameson paid the taxes for his sister Margaret Robinson because she had no money after paying for the warrant and interest due so that her family could stay on the land.

The Westmoreland County, Unity Township, census of 1790 shows that Margaret Robinson has in the household one free white male of 16+, including Head of Family, and three free white males under 16, and four free white females, including Head of Family. Samuel would have been the one free white male, and the daughter named Margaret would have been married and not counted in the family.

Then on March 18, 1793, Margaret transferred 167½ acres of land to her son Samuel Robinson, who would have been over twenty-one years old at the time, for five shillings. As per the law at the time, she could not own property, including land. From the document, it looks like the state had taken over the land on September 7, 1790. Margaret divided the property into nine portions. Samuel received two portions, and her other children—Mary, Margaret, Isabella, Rosanna, Francis, David, and John Jr.—each received one portion. Samuel was to hold the portions for each heir until they reached the age of twenty-one years old. That meant the complete estate would not be settled until John Jr. was twenty-one years old, in 1803.

The deed was signed on March 18, 1793, between Margaret Robinson and Samuel Robinson and indicates that she was still an unmarried widow at the time. This was done to settle the estate of John Robinson just prior to her marriage to John Peoples. The marriage date between Margaret Jameson Robinson and John Peoples was in 1794, which also is prior to the birth of their daughter Margaret Jane Peoples in 1795.

Margaret Robinson Property, 1786

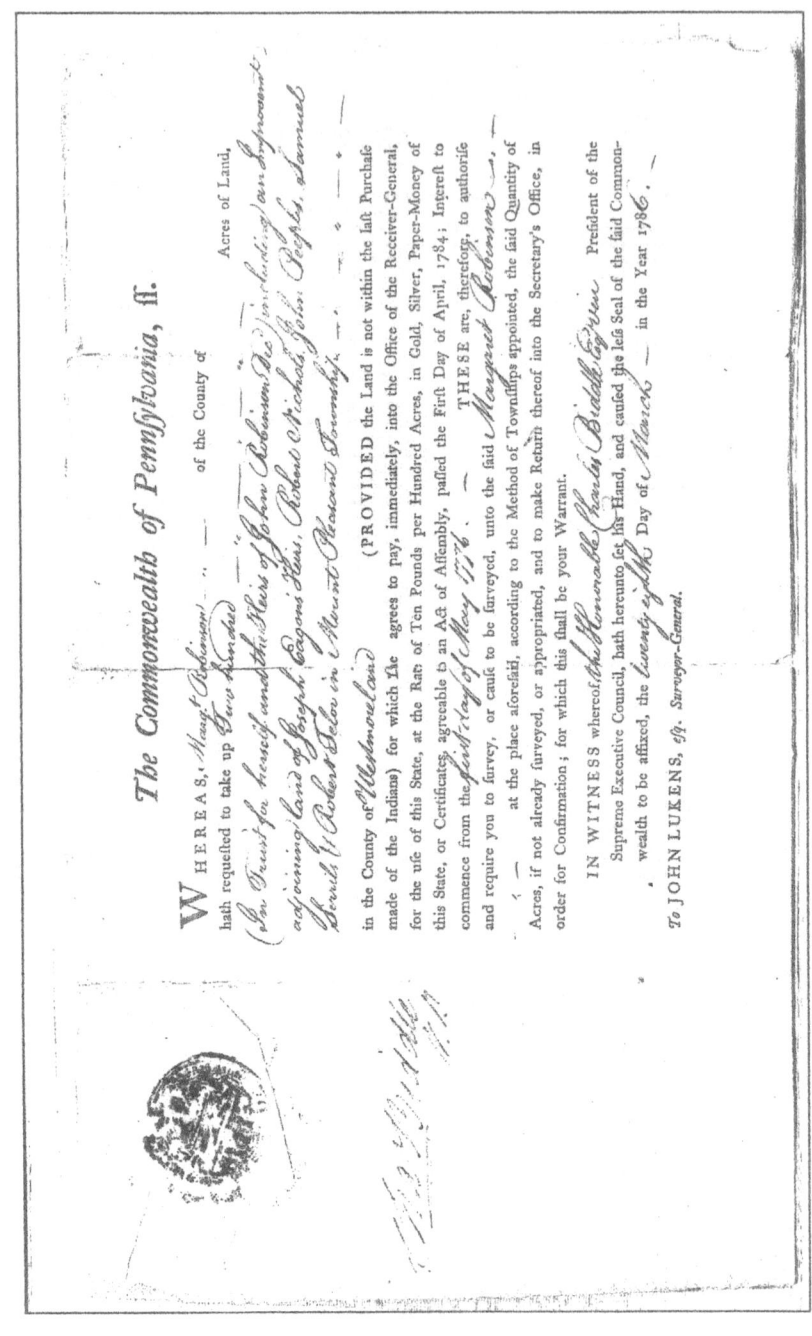

Margaret Robinson, Land Warrant 1786
This is the application for "Margareta" that Margaret had filed.

Land Transfer from Margaret Robinson to Samuel Robinson[7]

Know all men by these presents that Margaret Robinson of Westmoreland County in the state of Pennsylvania widow for divers good causes and considerations and also for and in consideration <u>of the sum of five shillings</u> lawful money of the state aforesaid tome in hand well and truly paid by Samuel Robinson of the county and state aforesaid my eldest son by John Robinson of the country aforesaid deceased my late husband the receipt and payment whereof is hereby fully acknowledged save and granted bargained sold alluded released and confirmed and by these presents do grant bargain sell release and confirm unto him the said Samuel Robinson his heirs and assigns all that certain plantation or tract of land situate on the harbors severely in <u>Mount Pleasant Township</u> in the county aforesaid beginning at a white oak hence by land of John Wofhart south thirty seven degrees east one hundred and thirteen perches to a white oak hence by manor land south eighty two degrees east one hundred and fifty four perches to a walnut hence north eighty four degrees east sixty two perches to a port hence by land of William Eager north fifteen degrees west one hundred and thirty perches to a hickory thence by land of Robert Nichols north eighty seven degrees west one hundred and twenty five perches to a white oak and thence by land of John Peoples south seventy eight degrees west one hundred and twenty seven perches to the place of beginning containing one hundred and sixty seven acres and an half and allowance etc. with the appurtenances it being <u>the same tract of land which the late supreme executive bonus of the said state by their patent bearing did the seventh day of September in the year of our Lord one thousand seven hundred and ninety</u> for the consideration therein expressed die grant unto me the said Margaret Robinson my heirs and assigns as by the said patent enrolled in the rolls office for the said state in patent book no. 15, page 330 reference being thereunto had more fully will appear to have and to hold the said described plantation and tract of land situate lying and containing as

aforesaid called in the said patent Margareta and premises hereby granted mentioned or intended so to be with the appurtenances unto him the <u>said Samuel Robinson his heirs and assigns in trust for himself and Mary Margaret Rosanna Isabel Francis David and John the other and remaining children of the aforesaid John Robinson deceased as here after mentioned and described to wit to the proper use and benefit of him the said Samuel Robinson two shares or parts and to the aforesaid Mary Margaret Rosanna Isabel Francis David and John each one share the whole plantation or tract of land aforesaid with its appurtenances in nine equal shares or parts supposed to be divided and to no other use whatsoever the said Samuel Robinson to stand seized and possessed of the aforesaid plantation and premises and interest therein before mentioned until the youngest child or surviving child shall attain the age of twenty one years when the above named children or their legal representatives shall be respectively entitled to hold their several shares and interest therein as aforesaid in their own rights or at their pleasure to sell and dispose of the same</u> in witness whereof I have hereunto set my hand and seal this eighteenth day of March in the year of our lord one thousand seven hundred ninety three.
Sealed and delivered - Margaret [her X mark] Robinson [seal] in the presence of
Thomas Hamelton, John Peebles
Received on the day of the date of the foregoing instrument of writing the sum of five shillings from the above-named Samuel Robinson being the consideration money therein mentioned.
Witness present - Margaret [her X mark] Robinson [seal]
Thomas Hamelton, John Peoples
Westmoreland County SS
Personally, came before me the subscriber one of the Justices of the Peace in and for the county of Westmoreland aforesaid the within named Margaret Robinson the grantor in the within deed mentioned and acknowledged the same to be her own properties and deed in order that the same may be recorded as such. Witness my hand and seal the same eighteenth day of

March in the year last within written.
[seal] Robert Taylor
Recorded April 3rd, 1793.
==
PA State Archives, Land Records Roll No. 1.16, Patent Indexes (p. 268) says:
P-No. 15 -
Date of Patent = 7 Sept. 1790
Where recorded = page 330
Patentee = Margaret Robinson
Area = 167 acres, 80 prs.
Warrantee = Margaret Robinson
Name of Tract = Margareta
Date of Warrant = 28 March 1786
County = Westmoreland

Margaret Robinson, 1786 Land Transfer, Warrant for "Margareta"

FORM No. 1.

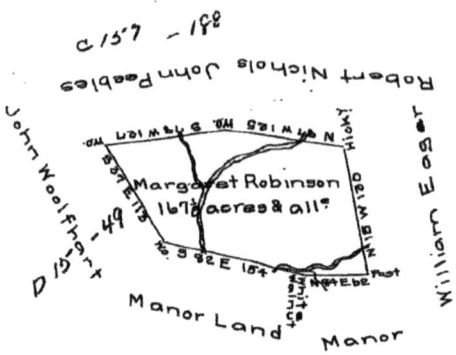

In pursuance of a warrant bearing date March 28th 1786 surveyed on the 15th day of June 1788 unto Margaret Robinson the above discribed tract of land situate on the waters of Sewickley — in Mount Pleasant township in the County of Westmoreland containing one hundred and sixty seven acres and allowce of six per cent for roads &c.

Benj Lodge D.S.

To John Lukens Esqr }
Surveyor General }

IN TESTIMONY that the above is a copy of the original remaining on file in the Department of Internal Affairs of Pennsylvania, made conformably to an Act of Assembly approved the 16th day of February, 1855, I have hereunto set my Hand and caused the Seal of said Department to be affixed at Harrisburg, this twentieth *day of* July *1906.*

Secretary of Internal Affairs.

Land Survey with drawn description, dated March 28, 1786; surveyed on 15th of June 1788

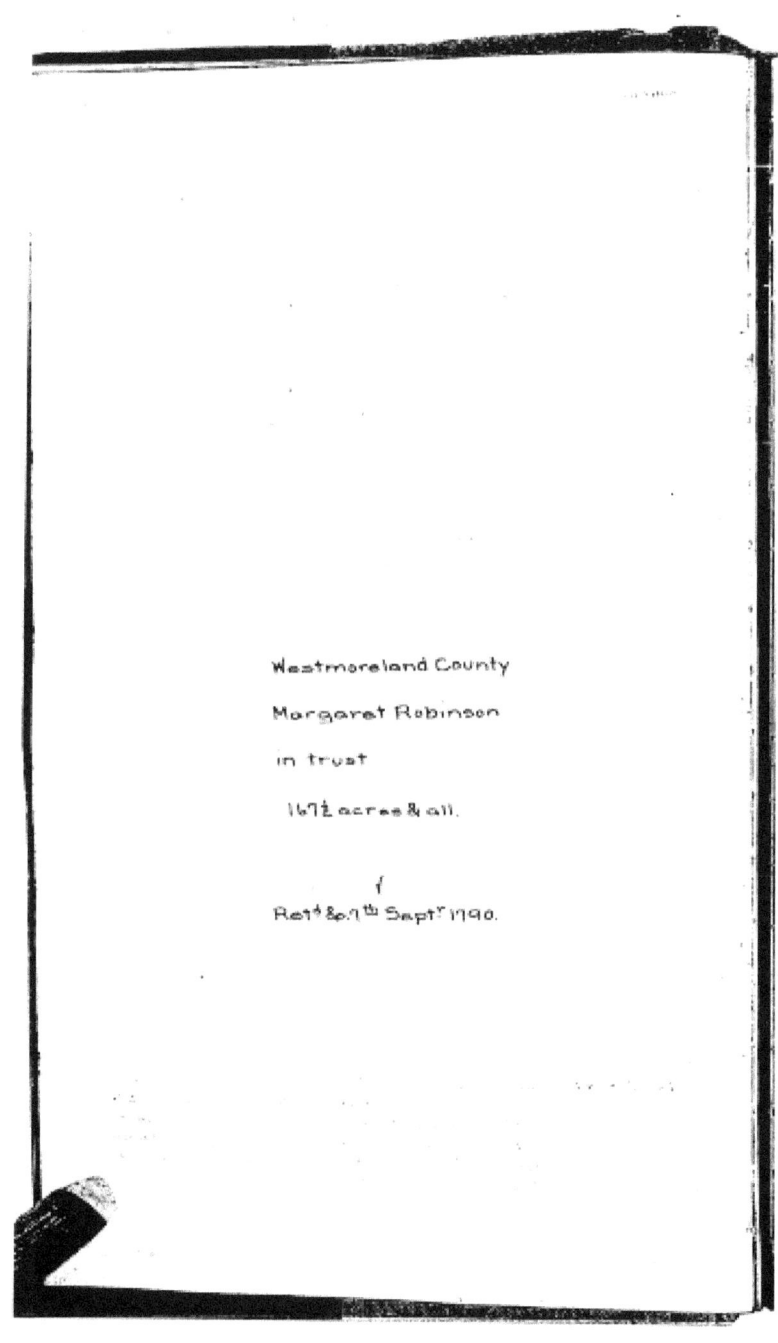

"Westmoreland County Margaret Robinson in trust 167½ acres & all."
7th Sept 1790

Margaret Robinson Patent 1786

1786 Pennsylvania State and County Tax & Exoneration List

After the transfer of the "Margareta" property, Margaret married neighbor John Peoples in Westmoreland County, Pennsylvania, in 1794. John Peoples had the property adjoining the John and Margaret Robinson property.

Margaret had a child with John Peoples. The child was named Margaret Jane Peoples and was born in 1795.** Later in life, Margaret Jane Peoples married John Reed. She died on April 15, 1880.

John Peoples died in 1797, three years after his marriage to Margaret Robinson. He was "very sick and weak" as noted in his will.

The following is the will summary for John Peoples from the Will Abstract in Old Westmoreland County and some other documents related to the marriage of Margaret Robinson and John Peoples.[8]

JOHN PEOPLES (also **PEEBLES**), farmer. "Very sick and weak." Wife: Margaret. Son: William. Daughters: "Elizabeth, Mary, Agnes, and Margaret Jane." Also mentions David **ROBINSON**. Also mentions his plantation. Executors: John **NICKLAS** and Robert **NICKLAS**. Witnesses: John **BAIRD**, Robert **JAMISON**, and Robert (x) **ROBESON**. Will dated 16 Dec 1797, proved 22 Dec 1797.

** The identification of Margaret Jane Peoples as a child from John Peoples second marriage (to Margaret Jameson Robinson) is based upon her being very young and taking direct care of Margaret Jameson Robinson in her old age. Also, in the future Margaret Peoples is given land by her half brothers, Samuel and Francis Robinson, and her future husband would inherit property from Margaret Robinson

The following deed dated December 28, 1801, is for the sale of 100 acres for eight hundred pounds, to be paid to Samuel, Margaret, Rosanna, David, and Isabel Robinson. Missing from this sale is Mary and Francis. John was not twenty-one years old at the time, so Samuel was his trustee.[9]

ADAM HARTZEL & JOHN HARTZEL
TO THE HEIRS OF JOHN ROBINSON DE[C]EASED

Know all men by these presents that we Adam Hartzel and John Hartzel both of Westmoreland County and state of Pennsylvania are held and firmly bound unto Samuel Robinson, John Johnston and Margaret his wife, Rosanna Robinson, David Johnston and Isabel his wife, Francis Robinson, David Robinson, and John Robinson, surviving children & heirs of John Robinson late of the country aforesaid deceased in <u>the sum of eight hundred pounds</u> lawful money of Pennsylvania to be paid to the said Samuel Robinson, John Johnston & Margaret his wife, Rosanna Robinson, David Johnston and Isabel his wife, Francis Robinson, and John Robinson as to their certain attorney executors administrators or assigns to which payment well and truly to be paid we do bind ourselves and each of us and each our heirs executors and administrators & every of them jointly and severally for and in the whole family by these presents sealed with our seals dated <u>the twenty eighth day of December in the year of our Lord one thousand eight hundred and one,</u> whereas the above named several heirs of John Robinson by an indenture under the hand and seals bearing even date with these presents for the consideration therein mentioned did grant and confirm part of their land to the above named Adam Hartzel his heirs and assigns <u>containing one hundred acres</u> strict measure as in and by the said indenture may appear, and whereas the said Adam Hartzel has already made a mill race through and a small dam on a part of the land to him sold as aforesaid and will probably enlarge and extend the said dam across the bottom above the meadow ground belonging to the other lands of said heirs for the better conveying the water on his mill to more advantage whereby it is likely said meadow might some time or other be damaged if not due care be taken, wherefore the condition of the above obligation is such that if the above Adam Hartzel his heirs executors & administrators & every of these shall and will from time to time and at all times hereafter well and sufficiently save keep harmless and indemnify the said above named heirs of the said John Robinson deceased their heirs executors & administrators respectively or whomsoever they transfer the residue of their land to whereon the said meadow ground loss from all damages & spoilation's the said dam and race shall or any occasion thereon and from all actions suits payments debts charges & damages for or by reason thereof then the above obligation to be void and of non-feel otherwise to be and remain in full force & virtue in law.

Sealed and delivered in the presence of John Baird, James White
Adam Hartzel [seal]
John Hartzel [seal]

+++

The following is an interesting document regarding the sale of approximately 96 acres in Mount Pleasant Township, Westmoreland County. Samuel Robinson, Rosanna Robinson, and Francis Robinson sold the 96 acres to John Chambers for 386 pounds. Samuel had purchased 27 acres of land of the Sewickley Manor on April 25, 1794. His siblings, John Robinson, David Robinson, and Margaret Robinson gave up their right to the Sewickley Manor tract on a quit claim dated December 1801 to Samuel Robinson, Rosanna Robinson, Francis Robinson, and Isabella Robinson.

Rosanna, Isabella, and Francis released their rights to Samuel on March 27, 1804. Mary died prior to this date.

The following is a summary of the deed dated May 13, 1805:[10]

13 May 1805. Deed. Samuel ROBINSON, David GARDNER and Rosanna Robinson, his wife, and Francis ROBINSON, surviving children and heirs to John ROBINSON of Westmoreland Country dec's, to John CHAMBERS of Unity Twp, blacksmith. <u>Price: lb386.</u> Land: Messuage, tenement, and two tracts of land adjoining each other, situated in Unity twp. with and buildings and improvements thereon: 1) <u>69 acres 52 1/4 perches</u> bounded by Adam HARTZEL, William MOOMYERS, heirs of John TREMBEL, --- POORMAN, and the Manor line; it being part of 16 1/2 acres, called "Margarita", which Margaret ROBINSON (then widow and relict of the deceased) by deed 18 Mar 1993 (Westmoreland Country Deed Book 1, page 380) sold to Samuel ROBINSON in trust for the use of the several surviving heirs of the deceased. 2) <u>27 acres 23 1/8 perches</u>, bounded by --- POORMAN, said CHAMBER's other land, and the previous tract; it being part of a tract of Manor land (called Sewickley Manor) which Christian LAFFER and Sarah his wife 25 Apr 1794 (Westmoreland County Deed Book 2, page 100) sold to Samuel ROBINSON. And whereas the other heirs of said John ROBINSON, viz: John JOHNSTON and Margaret his wife, David ROBINSON, and John ROBINSON and Sarah his wife, by release -- Dec 1801 quit claimed their rights in the land to Samuel ROBINSON, Rosanna ROBINSON (since intermarried to the said David GARDNER), David JOHNSTON and Isabel his wife, and Francis ROBINSON. And whereas David JOHNSTON and Isabel his wife by an assignment underneath the said release, dated 27 Mar 1804, released their rights to said lands to Samuel ROBINSON. Witnesses: Robert JAMISON and William MOMEYER. (Page 177)

The following is the deed of sale for Sewickley Manor, May 13, 1805. Samuel, Rosanna, and Francis Robinson sold the land for 386 pounds.[11]

DOCUMENT: Samuel Robinson to John Chambers

This indenture made the thirteenth day of May in the year of our Lord one thousand eight hundred and five <u>between Samuel Robinson, David Gardner and Rosanna his wife, and Francis Robinson, surviving children and heirs of John Robinson late of Westmoreland Country and State of Pennsylvania deceased</u> of the one part and John Chambers of Unity Township in the country and state aforesaid blacksmith of the other part witnesseth that the said Samuel Robinson, David Gardner and Rosanna his wife, and Francis Robinson, for a consideration of <u>the sum of three hundred and eighty six pounds</u> lawful current money of Pennsylvania to them in hand will and truly paid by the said John chambers at or before the ensealing and delivery of these presents the receipt whereof they do hereby acknowledge and thereof acquit and forever discharge the said John Chambers, his heirs, executors, and administrators have and each of them hath granted, bargained, sold, alieved, enfeoffed, released, and confirmed, and by these presents do and each of them hath granted, bargained, sell aliened, enfeoff, released, and conferred unto the said John Chambers and to his heirs and assigns all that the following described hereditaments and two pieces of land adjoining each other situate in Unity Township Westmoreland County aforesaid the one beginning at a post in line of said Chambers land thence north eighty degrees west twenty five and a half perches to a post thence by Adam Hartzel land north eight degrees west thirty nine perches to a post thence by William Mooneyers land north seventy eight degrees east one hundred and seventy perches and five licks to a post thence by heirs of John Tremble south fifteen degrees east one hundred and one perch to a post thence by Poormans land north eighty nine degrees west to a white walnut thence by the Manor line north eighty two degrees west ... perches to beginning containing sixty nine acres fifty two perches and one fourth of land and allowance of land the other of said pieces of land beginning at the aforementioned white walnut in said Poormans land thence south twenty four degrees west fifty three perches to a black oak south one degree west thirty four perches to a black walnut thence by said Chambers other land north sixty five degrees west forty five perches to a white oak north twenty two degrees west seventy nine perches to the place of beginning containing twenty seven acres twenty three perches and one eighth of land both said pieces of land containing agreeable to a survey lately made ninety six acres and seventy six and a half perches of land with usual allowance of six per lot for roads H ... [the first of the foregoing described pieces of land being a part of a certain tract of one hundred and sixty seven and a half acres of land & allowance called Margarita and which Margaret Robinson then the widow and relict of the said John Robinson deceased by her deeds poll dated the eighteenth day of March in the year one thousand seven hundred and ninety three for the consideration and reservations therein mentioned did grant and convey unto the said Samuel Robinson & to his heirs and assigns in trust for the use and benefit of the several surviving heirs of the said deceased as in and by the said deed poll recorded in the office for recording of deeds in and for the country of Westmoreland in >>> reference thereunto being had more fully and at large appears and the other not last of the above described pieces of land being a part of a certain tract of Manor land (called Sewickley Manor) which a certain Christian (page 178) Laffer and Sarah his wife by an indenture under their hands and seals executed dated the twenty fifth day of April in the year one thousand seven hundred and ninety four for the consideration therein mentioned did grant and convey unto the said Samuel Robinson his heirs and assigns forever as in and by the said indenture likewise recorded in the aforesaid office in >>> H. reference thereunto had more fully may appear and whereas the other heirs of said John Robinson namely John Johnston and Margaret his wife, David

Robinson, John Robinson and Sarah his wife, by their release in the month of December 1801 for the consideration therein mentioned did each of them for themselves their heirs etc. respectively by grant bargain sell remise release and forever quit claim unto the aforesaid Samuel Robinson, Rosanna Robinson (since intermarried to a David Gardner, David Johnston and Isabel his wife, and Francis Robinson, all and singular their respective shares right title claim and demand to the above described two pieces of land premises and appurtenances thereunto belonging to hold the same to them their heirs and assigns forever as in and by the said release may appear and whereas the said David Johnston and Isabel his wife by an assignment underneath the said release dated the twentieth seventh day of March 1804 for the consideration therein mentioned did release assign all his right & title to said land and premises unto the said Samuel Robinson his heirs and assigns forever as in and by the said assignment appears] Together with all and singular the buildings improvements ways woods waters water courses rights liberties privileges hereditaments and appurtenances to each of the said pieces of land belonging or in any ways appertaining & the reversions and remainders rents issues and profits thereof and also all the estate right title interest property claim and demand whatsoever of them the said Samuel Robinson (as well for himself as for David Johnston and Isabel his wife) David Gardner & Rosanna his wife, and Francis Robinson and each and every of them of in to or out of the same and every part thereof in law or equity to have and to hold the said messuage or tenement and two pieces of land hereditaments and premises hereby granted or mentioned or intended so to be unto the said John Chambers his heirs and assigns to be only proper use and behoof of the said John Chambers his heirs and assigns forever and the said above named grantors for themselves & their respective heirs executors and administrators do and each of them doth covenant promise grant and agree to and with said John Chambers his heirs and assigns by these presents that they the above named grantors and their heirs the said above mentioned and described messuage and two pieces of land hereditaments and premises hereby granted mentioned or intended so to be with the appurtenances unto the said John Chambers his heirs and assigns against them the above within named grantors and their respective heirs and against all and every other person and persons whomsoever lawfully claiming or to claim by from or under them or any or either of them shall and will warrant and forever defend in witness whereof the said parties to these have hereunto interchangeably set their hands and seals the day and year within written.

Samuel Robinson [seal]
David Gardner [seal]
Rosanna [her mark] Robinson [seal]
Francis [his mark] Robinson [seal]
Sealed and delivered in presence of us. Robert Jamison, William Monuger.
Received on the day of the date of the above indenture from John Chamber and sum of three hundred and eighty-six pounds being in full the consideration money within mentioned.
Samuel Robinson
David Gardner
Francis [his mark] Robinson
Witnesses present at signing. Robert Jamison, William Monuger.

Westmoreland County SS Before me the subscribed one of the Justices of the Peace in and for said country personally came Samuel Robinson, David Gardner and Isabel his wife, and Francis Robinson the grantors above mentioned and acknowledged the foregoing indenture to be their act and deed and desired that the same might be recorded as such the said Rosanna being of full age apart from her said husband by me examined the contents thereof being first made known unto her she voluntarily consented thereunto. In witness whereof I have hereunto set my hand & seal the thirteenth day of May AD 1805.
Recorded February 15th, 1808. Hugh Martin [seal]

Then in 1806 or 1807, Margaret and Samuel Robinson moved to Buffalo Township in Armstrong County, Pennsylvania. This is based on the Tax Assessment of 1807, Buffalo Township, Armstrong County, Pennsylvania:[12]

    Margaret Peoples (widow) – Buffalo Township
    Samuel Robinson – Buffalo Township

On June 13, 1810, William Findley sold land to Margaret Peoples that is adjacent to the lands of Samuel Robinson and Francis Robinson, her sons.[13]

This document is witnessed by *both* Robert Robinson's. The signing date is 13 June 1810. The land is adjacent to Samuel Claypole. This indicates that Margaret (nee Jameson; widow Robinson) Peoples moved to Armstrong Co. with at least two of her sons, Samuel and Francis. What makes this interesting is that her deceased husband's brother, Robert Robinson, is still in her life and helping her out on this purchase of property.

The 1820, the Buffalo Township, Armstrong County, Pennsylvania Census shows that Margaret along with her sons Samuel and John are living there. The widow Margaret Peoples appears in the 1820 Armstrong County census as one 26-45 male, one 16-21 female, and one 45+ female.[14]

Peoples, Margaret
    1820 census, BUFFALO TWP page 297
Robinson, John
    1820 census, BUFFALO TWP page 298
Robinson, Samuel
    1820 census, BUFFALO TWP page 297

On March 3, 1821, William Findley sells some land to Samuel Robinson and Francis Robinson [Samuel Robinson al grantee, Wm Findley grantor][15] William Findley of Unity Township, Westmoreland, County, Pennsylvania, sells land to Samuel Robinson and Francis Robinson of Buffalo Township, Armstrong County, Pennsylvania. This agreement was signed on 7 November 1806 and finally recorded in March 1821.

On April 24, 1821, Samuel Robinson transferred property to Margaret Jane Peoples, his stepsister. This document also mentions brother Francis

Robinson. The land is said to be part of the William Findley track. The sale itself was on April 4, 1821. Witnessed by David Johnston (brother-in-law of the Robinsons) and Sally Jack (sister-in-law of Samuel Robinson).[16]

On November 11, 1831, Margaret Robinson Peoples gave land to her widowed daughter-in-law, Sarah Robinson, widow of John Jr., via son Samuel Robinson and Francis Robinson.

> Adjoining "Strabane" on the east in a large scope of apparently unsurveyed territory or blank space on the Gapen map, is on the other depreciation lot No. 276, in shape a rectangular parallelogram, for which, called "Unequal Contest", the patent was granted to William Findley, November 20, 1786, as <u>containing 276 3/10 acres, which he conveyed to Margaret Peebles, April 24, 1821, for $200. Samuel Robinson then released 121 acres to Francis Robinson, November 3, 1821, for five shillings, who conveyed the same to Sarah Robinson (widow of John Jr., who died in 1831), November 11, 1831, for $1.</u>

Then on April 7, 1833, Margaret Robinson Peoples purchased 100 acres for $150 and then sold the property to John Reed for $5 for the "purpose of Margaret Robinson Peoples perpetual care." John Reed was the husband of Margaret's daughter, Margaret Jane Peoples.[17]

> Adjoining "Lamie Bay" on the west is depreciation lot No. 277, 201 acres called "Out-lot", the patent for which was granted to William Lindley, November 20, 1786, for £5, who conveyed one-half of it to Margaret Peebles (who was first assessed in Buffalo township with 1 horse and 2 cows in 1806 at $32), adjoining her other land on which she then resided and including "an improvement made by Samuel Claypoole" where he then resided, June 30, 1810, for $150, which she conveyed to John Reed, October 30, 1833, for $5, "natural love and affection", and his covenant to maintain her during the rest of her life" in such a manner as a woman of her age requires", and to afford her a proper Christian burial.[18]

Margaret Robinson and her children Samuel, John, and Isabella lived for about a decade just to the north of Cowansville.

Margaret Jameson Robinson Peoples died in October 1837, having lived a long life of eighty-nine years. There is a Robinson buried next to Margaret, but the headstone is illegible. Margaret is buried at Cowansville Presbyterian Church Cemetery in Armstrong County, Pennsylvania.

Margaret Robinson Peoples, Headstone
"In the 89th Year of Her Age."

THE JOURNEY FORWARD

JENNIE & THOMAS

Jennie Robinson was born August 28, 1740. The nickname of Jennie is a derivative of the formal name Jane; therefore, Jennie may have been recorded on her birth record as Jane Robinson. She was the twin sister to John Robinson. Her father and mother were twenty-one years old and twenty years old, respectively, at the time of her birth.

She emigrated with her parents from Maghera, Londonderry County, Ireland, and arrived at the port of Philadelphia, Pennsylvania, on October 25, 1771. Upon arriving in British America, she and her parents traveled west to the family plantation in Lancaster County, Pennsylvania.

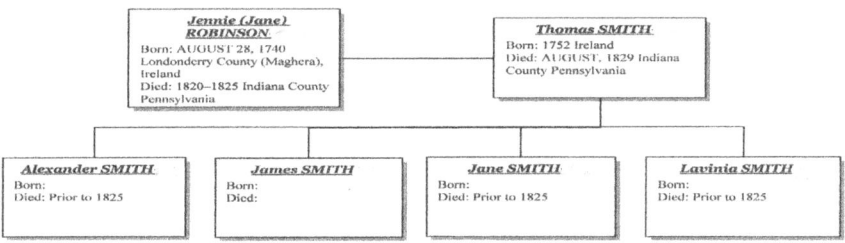

Jennie Robinson Smith Family Chart

Later, she met and married Thomas Smith at the Conocoheague (Conikakig) Settlement in Pennsylvania. Thomas Smith, the pioneer, who wove clothing at the Conocoheague Settlement and was also a farmer. Both were natives of Ireland. After a few years, Thomas sold his farm at the Settlement for Continental money, but the transaction proved utterly worthless. It was at this juncture the family moved to Westmoreland County.

By the end of 1778, Continental money retained from one-fifth to one-seventh of its face value. By 1780, the bills were worth only one-fortieth of their face value. Congress attempted to reform the currency by removing the old bills from circulation and issuing new ones, without success. By May 1781, the Continentals had become so worthless that they ceased to circulate as money.

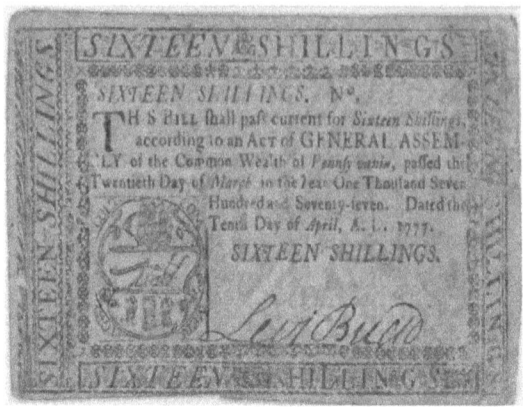

Continental Money

In mid-1778, Jennie Robinson Smith and her family migrated west with her brothers and sister to near the present site of Youngstown, Westmoreland County, Pennsylvania. Youngstown was originally referred to as Martinsburg. Until 1796, it had been randomly settled, with various people making claims to the land. The first recorded land transaction was made on March 31, 1796. The Robinson-Smith family settled in the area called the "Big Road," which referred to the Forbes Trail, located near Youngstown, Pennsylvania *(see map, p. 31).*

Then about 1795, Jennie, Thomas, and their children moved to Armstrong Township in Westmoreland County to a seventy-five-acre plantation (Armstrong Township became Conemaugh Township, Indiana County in 1803). This plantation was eventually handed down to their grandson Thomas who lived out his life on the family plantation. The plantation was in the same county and southeast of Jennie's brother Robert's plantation.

The children of Jennie and Thomas Smith were Alexander, James, Jane, and Lavina. Thomas died in August 1829, and Jennie died sometime between August 7, 1820, the date of the 1820 Census, and before October 1825. Thomas Smith's will is dated October 1825 and has no mention of Jennie in the document. Alexander, Jane, and Lavinia had most likely died prior to 1825 too, since James was the only child mentioned in the Thomas Smith will.

There is very little information known about Jennie's life after her marriage, which would be typical for this period.

LAVINA & SAMUEL

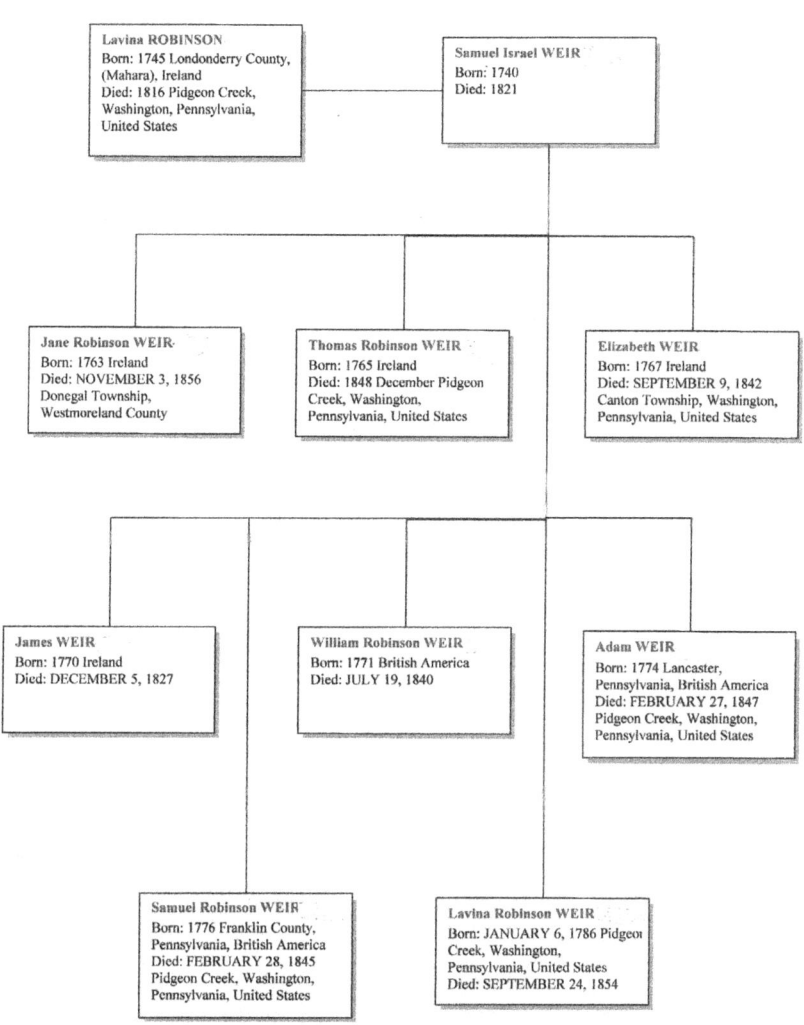

Lavina Robinson Weir Family Chart

Lavina (nickname Levey) Robinson Weir was born in 1745 in Ireland. She was the youngest daughter of Robert and Isabella Harris Robinson. Her father and mother were twenty-five years old and twenty-four years old, respectively, at the time of her birth.

Levey married Samuel Weir, who was born in 1740 in Londonderry County, Ireland. They were married in 1765 in Ireland prior to sailing to British America. Samuel Weir is the younger brother of Rachel Weir Robinson, wife of Robert Robinson.

Throughout this journey, Samuel and Levey stayed close with her older brother Robert Robinson and Samuel's older sister Rachel Robinson and their family. *"These families remained near each other, tarrying to Lancaster and Dauphin counties, finally proceeding to Big Sewickley, Westmoreland County."*[1]

Lavina emigrated with her husband and four children from Maghera, Londonderry County, Ireland, along with numerous other Weir family members and arrived at the port of Philadelphia, Pennsylvania, British America, on July 25, 1770, on the ship named the *Phoenix*. Upon arriving in British America, they traveled west with Robert and Rachel Robinson to Lancaster County, Pennsylvania.

Altogether they had eight children: Jane (Robinson), Thomas, Elizabeth, James, William, Adam, Samuel, and Lavina (Erwin).

Jane Weir Robinson

Jane was born in 1763 in Ireland and married her cousin James Robinson. She died on November 3, 1856, in Donegal, Westmoreland County, Pennsylvania, at the age of eighty-three years.

Thomas Robinson Weir

Thomas was born in 1765 in Ireland; and he died in December 1848 at eighty-three years of age.

Elizabeth Weir

Elizabeth was born in 1767 in Ireland; and he died in Canton Township, Washington County, Pennsylvania, on September 9, 1842, at seventy-five years old. She had thirteen children.

James Weir
James was born in 1770 in Ireland; and he died December 5, 1827, at fifty-seven years of age.

William Robinson Weir
William was born in British America in 1771; he died on July 19, 1840, at the age of sixty-nine years.

Adam Weir
Adam was born in 1774 in Lancaster County, Pennsylvania; and he died February 27, 1847, at the age of seventy-three years.

"Yours as ever" Adam Weir

Samuel Robinson Weir

Samuel was born in 1776 and died on February 28, 1845, at the age of sixty-nine years of age on his father's farm, the original Weir homestead in West Bethlehem Township, Washington County, Pennsylvania. He was unmarried.

Lavina Robinson Weir (Erwin)
Lavina was born on January 6, 1786, and died September 24, 1854, at the age of sixty-eight years. She married James Erwin later in life, and they had no children.

The Weir family had lived with Robert and Rachel Robinson and helped with the farming on Robert's plantation since arriving at the Big Sewickley Settlement, Westmoreland County, in 1778.

But in 1781, after living at Big Sewickley Settlement for a few years, Samuel and Levey Weir decided to move to the vicinity of Zollarville, Washington County, Pennsylvania. Here they stayed for a while, but finally settled on Pigeon Creek, West Bethlehem Township, near the present-day town of Vanceville, Washington County, Pennsylvania. The distance was approximately forty-five miles from the Big Sewickley Settlement to Pigeon Creek. The trip would have taken about two to three days with wagons and pack horses.

THE WHISKEY REBELLION AND SAMUEL WEIR

The Whiskey Rebellion was a protest against the government having placed a high tax on whiskey, took place from 1791 to 1794 in Western Pennsylvania.

Although there is no direct evidence that Samuel Weir took part in the aggression and intimidation tactics used to protest the tax, there are five points that indicate Samuel would have been involved in some way in the resistance known as the Whiskey Rebellion.

First and foremost, Pigeon Creek, where Samuel Weir lived, was one of the epicenters of the uprising. In September and October 1791, there were several incidents of tar and feathering of tax collectors and law enforcement people. The village of Pigeon Creek was not very populated at this time.

Second, several of the leaders of the Rebellion were former officers during the American Revolutionary War. Samuel was a lieutenant in the Lancaster County Militia and would fit into that category.

Third, upon his death, there was a third-party inventory of his assets. This inventory showed that Samuel owned the equipment necessary to make whiskey.

Fourth, Samuel is unlikely to have paid the tax since the people involved in the Whiskey Rebellion were known to have destroyed the stills of those neighbors who did pay the tax.

Fifth, there is a receipt for the sale of a barrel of whiskey that Joseph Weir, Samuel's grandson, collected from the estate. Apparently, Samuel sold a barrel of whiskey that his grandson owned for $12, yet he never paid his grandson for the barrel of whiskey before his death. The original request for payment from the estate is shown.

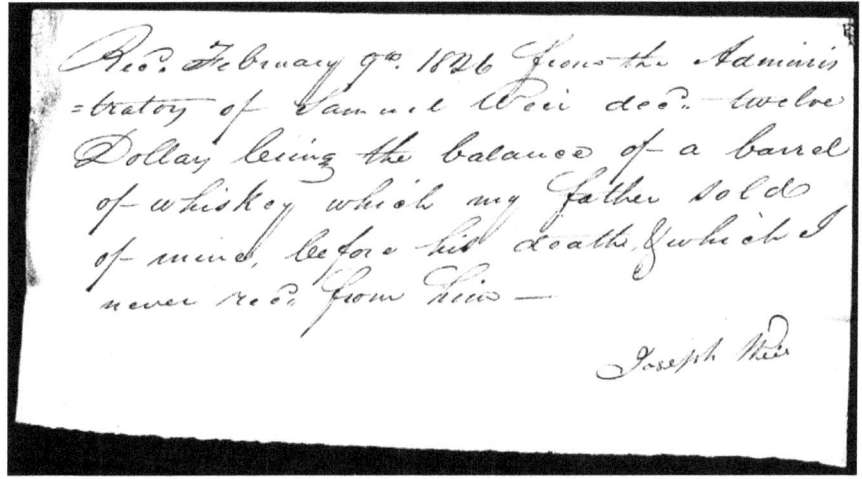

February 9, 1826, $12 Whiskey Debt

+++

Following the Revolutionary War and the creation of the U.S. Constitution, the federal government of the United States consolidated all war debts from each of the former colonies, now referred to as states. This mounting national debt required action, and Alexander Hamilton, the first Secretary of the Treasury, began establishing taxes in order to clear the nation's debts. Hamilton, believing that the newly established import duties were as high as they could be, decided that additional revenue was to be collected by the manufacture of whiskey. This new act taxed the manufacture of a product rather than the sale of a product and was the first federal tax on domestic products in the United States. Many Federalists believed that this new tax acted more of a "luxury tax" and did not have the ability to anger many citizens and therefore advocated its passing in Congress as the 1791 Excise Whiskey Tax. The 25 percent excise tax imposed on whiskey was presented as a luxury tax, but in the western frontier areas, whiskey was used as barter in place of the scarce currency issued by the new government.

Farmers in the backcountry saw the tax as an assault on their livelihood because it was easier and more profitable for farmers to convert their grain to whiskey before transporting it for sale to thirsty patrons in eastern markets. There was high demand for whiskey in early America. In the 1790s, Americans consumed nearly six gallons of alcohol per year, compared to just over two gallons today. Whiskey was almost the only source of ready cash in the nation's western regions and was a substitute for currency in many cases.

There were a greater number of stills and larger amount of whiskey manufactured in western Pennsylvania than in any other region of the same population in the whole country. **About every sixth man made whiskey, but all were involved in the problem, since the other five took their rye and corn to the stillhouse where the master distiller turned it into liquid form.** This is a very important statement regarding the production of whiskey in this region.

However, the Federalists failed to realize that whiskey production was held in high regard within the western frontier, specifically in western Pennsylvania. Many families that lived on the frontier relied on grain farming for food and income. Additionally, many grain farmers used the surplus grain to ferment and distill into whiskey in their home stills. Furthermore, many grain farmers preferred producing and trading whiskey rather than transporting and selling raw grain. Many families on the frontier used whiskey as a form of currency, as many traders and other frontiersmen did not have cash or other forms of money and so resorted to bartering and trading whiskey. Moreover, many grain farmers simply preferred the transportation of whiskey rather than raw grain, as many of the roads were poorly developed and whiskey could be transported longer than raw grain. Also, whiskey was more profitable than raw grain, and the frontiersmen could transport more whiskey than they could raw grain, so the whiskey trade was more appealing.

Many families on the frontier saw this tax as an affront to their livelihoods, as the whiskey trade was vital for their survival. As a result, many of these small family-owned distillery operations began to feel resentment

THE JOURNEY FORWARD

Whiskey Insurrection, Pennsylvania
"Famous Whiskey Insurrection in Pennsylvania," an 1880 illustration of a tarred-and-feathered tax collector being made to ride the rail.

against the current regime, believing that the George Washington administration was just as tyrannical as the English Parliament they had just fought to establish their own new and independent nations. Thus, protests began in western Pennsylvania against the perceived "elitist" tax as the stills in the frontier had to work harder to produce and transport their grain products for sale. The tax on whiskey was regressive, meaning that the more a distiller produced, the less they had to pay in taxes. The regressive nature of the tax disproportionately hurt the small distilleries owned by families on the frontier. Additionally, the tax was to be collected in cash, which many simply did not have on the frontier. This tax was poised to upset the entire market of bartering and trading that was established on the western frontier.

To protest the tax, those on the frontier simply refused to register their stills with the government. In order to combat the operation of unregistered stills, the federal government relied on local tax collectors and other locals to help locate the small stills on the frontier. As a result, many grain farmers and whiskey distillers lashed out at local "collaborators" and tax collectors, resorting to the tactics of the American Revolution. Tax collectors were being threatened and even tarred and feathered, all while public demonstrations became increasingly violent. Local militias were being formed for the purpose of fighting this tax.

The distillers in western Pennsylvania worked on a small scale and were hard pressed to afford the added tax, compared to larger operations located in eastern Pennsylvania. Frontier distillers reacted quickly and fiercely, organizing to resist the new tax, including many living along the banks of the Monongahela River in the southwest part of the state.

Yet, in no other place did popular fury rise so high, spread so rapidly, involve a whole population so completely, or express so many assorted grievances as in the Pennsylvania frontier counties of Fayette, Allegheny, Westmoreland, and Washington. There, in 1791, a light plume of wood smoke rose from no less than five thousand log stillhouses. The rates went into effect on July 1, 1791. The whiskey-maker could choose whether he would pay a yearly levy on his still capacity or a gallonage tax on his actual production.

On September 6, 1791, a mob, armed and disguised, attacked Robert Johnson, a tax collector for Allegheny and Washington counties, in Pigeon Creek, Washington County, Pennsylvania, and was subjected to local anger while out on his rounds. A gang of men—disguised with soot-blackened faces, bandannas, and women's clothing—attacked him. They took his horse, cut off his hair, and tarred and feathered him, stripping him of clothing and painfully covering him with hot tar and feathers. He managed to escape with his life and had to walk several miles to find help. Several people were proceeded against for the outrage, but the deputy marshal dared not serve the process, and if he had attempted it, he believes he would not have returned alive.

Shortly thereafter, another mob attacked John Connor, who was trying to arrest Robert Johnson's attackers. He was sent privately with the processes and was seized, whipped, tarred, and feathered. His money and horse were taken from him, and he was blindfolded and tied to a tree in the woods, where he remained for five hours.

The rebels were farmers angered by this federal excise tax on distilled liquors—the first direct tax on a domestic product in the nation's history. In the words of historian Jay Wink, the farmers "did far more than refuse to pay the infernal whiskey tax." Excisemen found themselves targets of musket balls, casualties of tarring and feathering, and victims of arson when the rebels burned their homes and businesses. Insurgents raised liberty poles to rally support, endorsed aggressive petitions, and established committees of correspondence to spread the word of their discontent. They destroyed the stills of neighbors who paid the tax. In short, they

President Washington and the Whiskey Rebellion

conducted themselves in the same manner that the American colonists did when resisting Parliament's taxes. To the rebels, they were the warriors who fought a revolution against a government imposing taxes unjustly. Their rebellion was a natural extension of the logic of the American Revolution.

George Washington called forth the militia to put down the rebellion and decided to take command himself. **This was the first and only time a sitting United States President ever led soldiers in an active campaign.**

By October of 1794, the federal army was closing the distance to Pittsburgh, resulting in the collapse of the rebellion, as many began to flee for safety from the massive federal force. The leaders of the insurrection fled into the frontier while the federal army began arresting suspected members of the rebellion.

When the dust had settled, approximately twenty people were indicted for their roles in the rebellion. Only ten people stood trial, however, and only two were convicted of treason. This was much to the dismay of Alexander Hamilton, who wanted to see more punitive measures taken against rebels to the United States. There followed several years of opposition to the payment of the whiskey tax and continued violence toward the collectors.

A large portion of the early settlers of western Pennsylvania were

Wagons and Whiskey Barrels

Scots-Irish and the remainder chiefly Germans, people whose early home, or that of their fathers, had been beyond the sea, in lands where whiskey, ale, or beer had been freely used and where excise laws and excise officers were regarded as "the most odious of all the measures and minions of tyranny." It can scarcely be wondered at, then, that among a people holding such opinions that the tax was regarded as most unjust and oppressive, nor that the more hot-headed and turbulent ones freely and fiercely announced their determination to oppose its enforcement, even to the extreme of armed resistance to the government.

Before the month of October was out, *"committees of correspondence,"* in the old Revolutionary phrase, were speeding horsemen over the ridges and through the valleys to arouse the people to arm and assemble. Many of the men who made the whiskey decided to "forbear" from paying the tax.

The Pennsylvania troubles were rooted in the economic importance and impregnable social position of mellow old Monongahela rye whiskey. The frontier people had been reared from childhood on the "family jug," and they found the taste pleasant, the effect agreeable. Whiskey kept the population cool in summer. In winter, it was the old settlers' equivalent of central heating. Whiskey was usually involved when there was kissing or fighting. It beatified the rituals of birth and death. It provided the only diversion, while enjoying at the same time a high reputation as the West's greatest therapeutic agent, effective against fevers, ague, snake bite, or general decline. The doctor kept a bottle in his office for his own use, with the protective label, "Arsenic—Deadly Poison."

In the end, George Washington combined his impressive show of force with an offer of amnesty to the rebels in exchange for an agreement to submit to the tax—perhaps in recognition that many of the disgruntled farmers had fought with him during the Revolutionary War. To show clemency and the fact that these two convicted traitors played a minimal role in the rebellion, President Washington pardoned the two convicted individuals during his Seventh State of the Union Address.

In late 1794, the Whiskey Rebellion disintegrated, and life returned to normal on the western frontier.

+++

The 1798 Washington County and Pennsylvania Tax List showed that Samuel Weir had 126 acres of land and one house on which he paid six hundred dollars in taxes. Also, it shows that his son Thomas was living on the plantation. Thomas would have been thirty-three years old at the time.

Samuel Weir officially became a citizen of the United States in September 1808 as described in the citizenship papers *(see p. 106)*.

Lavina Robinson Weir, his wife, died in 1816, at the age of seventy-one. Samuel died five years later. Very shortly after Samuel Weir died, the courts ordered "a true and perfect inventory and conscionable appraisement." This called for an exact and accurate inventory of his farm by a third party not associated with the family. This inventory showed that he had the equipment necessary to make whiskey. The inventory was dated May 4, 1821, which means that Samuel Weir died in early 1821.

The inventory taken after his death reports a significant amount of whiskey-making equipment on his property. This inventory shows evidence that Samuel Weir was in the production of whiskey as the final inventory of his property dated May 4, 1821, shows that he had an eighty-gallon still, a fifty-gallon still, five kegs, two barrels, eighteen still tubs, mills, and a cutting board. An interesting observation from the inventory after his death is that whiskey stills, barrels, and associated equipment for

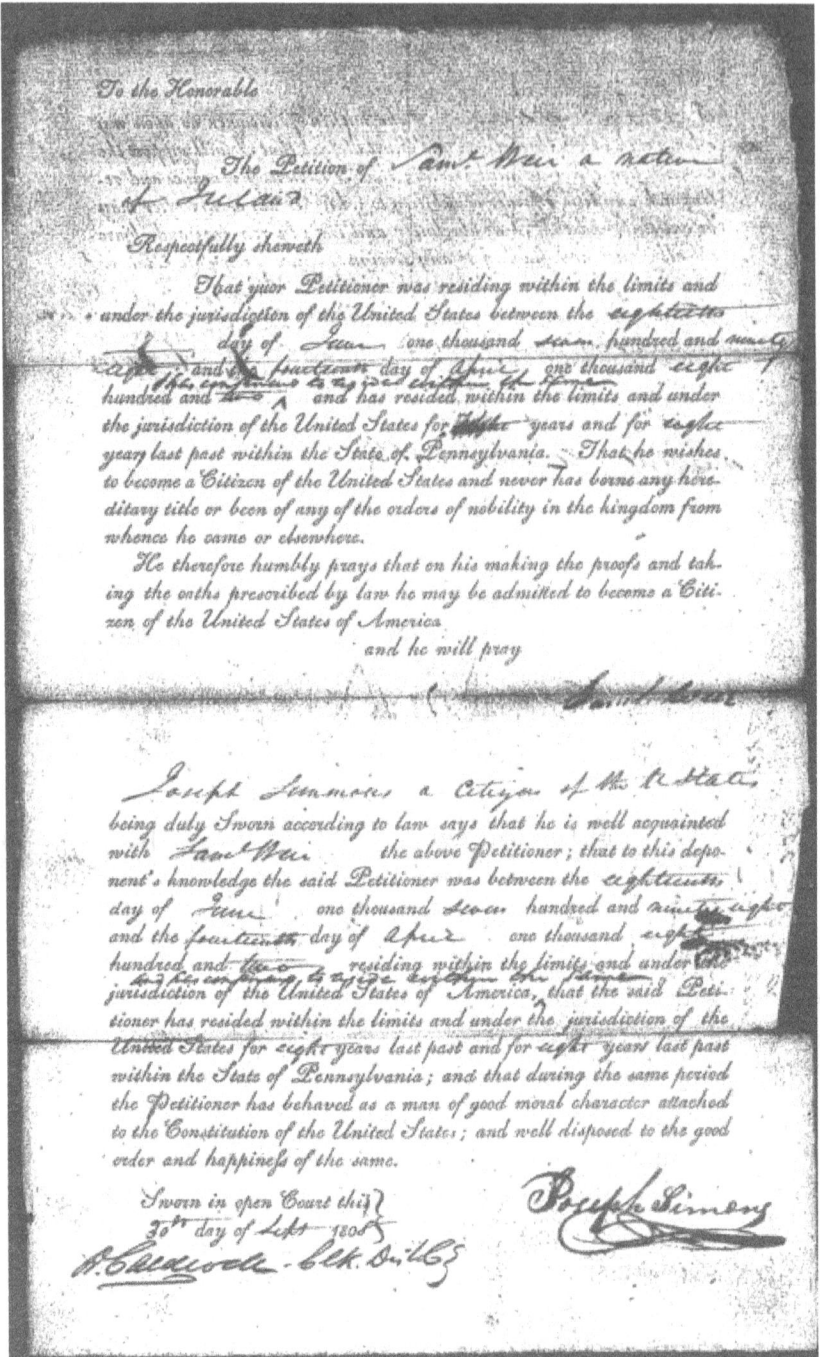

Citizenship Paper of Samuel Weir

whiskey manufacturing were valued more than the livestock. The inventory also implies that Samuel supported the Whiskey Rebellion since none of his equipment was destroyed in the rebellion as retribution for having paid the tax. All of this indicates that Samuel had been earning money by making and selling whiskey up until he died many years after the Whiskey Rebellion.

It is also likely that Samuel Weir was one of those not paying the whiskey excise tax and likely was a participant in the rebellion. There's no evidence that he was arrested for any of the rebellious activities, and his name does not appear on any documents that identify with people arrested and tried for their participation in the Whiskey Rebellion.

The final inventory also showed that he had loaned people money. There was one note dated April 1, 1820, for $115 plus interest and another noted dated March 27, 1820, for $24. The inventory showed that Samuel had $105 in cash in the house. This indicates that Samuel was one of the more prosperous farmers in the area, in that he could loan money to the other farmers.

A survey of the land was done on June 27, 1823, at a cost of $20 *(see land survey, p. 108)*.

+++

By 1820, Robert and Rachel Robinson were living with their son Capt. John Robinson. Even though Robert (brother of Lavina) and Rachel Robinson (sister of Samuel) were very close to Levey and Samuel Weir, because of age, health, and distance, they could no longer help each other.

Samuel Weir died in early 1821 at the age of eighty-one. Lavina (Levey) Robinson Weir and Samuel are buried in the Pigeon Creek Cemetery in Washington County, Pennsylvania.

In Samuel's will, Samuel Jr. inherited the plantation that his father and youngest sister Lavina were living on at the time of Samuel Sr.'s death. Lavina inherited one good mare saddle and bridle too. More significantly, the will states that Lavina (thirty-five years old at the time) should have the privilege to live on the plantation while she remained single, and that her brother Samuel was not to sell it without her consent until after she was married.

The Rights and Credits of Samuel Weir, Late of Washington County Deceased so far as laid before us this 4th Day of May 1821

	$	Cents
one Black & White Bull	10	00
one Black and White Cow & Calf	10	00
one Red and White Do.	11	00
one Red Do. and Calf	11	00
one Black heifer	7	00
one Black and White Do.	4	75
one Black steer with white face	7	50
one Black & white Do.	6	50
one Red & white Do.	8	50
one Red Cow with White face and Calf	10	50
one Do. Black white Spots	8	00
one Do. Red and White and Calf	8	00
one Black steer with white face	15	00
one Do. brindled with White face	13	00
one two year old steer	4	50
one Do.	4	00
one two year old heifer	4	50
one Do.	4	00
Six year old Calves	16	50
Twenty one head of Sheep & two Lambs	20	00
Twenty Head of Hogs	18	50
one Eighty Gallon Still	24	00
one old fifty Gallon Still and an additional Head	10	00
Three Kiggs	1	25
Two empty Barrels	0	62½
Eighteen old Still Tubbs	4	50
Jeune hands	1	25
one Wash one	5	50
one Cutting Box	1	00
two pitch and one Dung fork	0	56¼
Eight Barrels of flower	12	00
two old flake Stands	0	50
Lot old Barrels	1	00
Twenty two Bags	5	00
Lot of small gospel	0	62½
two Washing tubs an Slop Buckets	1	00

Samuel Weir, Land Survey, May 4, 1821
A survey of the land was done on June 27, 1823, at a cost of $20.

Headstone of Samuel Weir and Lavina Robinson Weir
"From Londonderry Co. Ireland 1770."

Adam Weir inherited the plantation he was currently living on and had to pay his youngest sister, Lavina, $106.67 immediately. Also, an interesting statement that reads that the executors "named execute unto him (Adam Weir) one good deed poll for the same." A "deed poll" is a legal document binding a single person, in this case Adam Weir. It is a deed and not a contract because it only binds one party.

Samuel Weir's final will was signed on October 10, 1817, and probated on April 16, 1821 *(see Will Book #3, p. 111).*

Lavina married James Erwin later. Her brother Samuel Robinson Weir never married. He died on the plantation on February 28, 1845.

A document dated 1825 shows Samuel Robinson Weir as the executor of the will for his father, Samuel Weir, along with Joseph Lawrence, a neighbor *(see 1825 Account, p. 110).*

The final estate settlement dated March 22, 1826, shows that the estate had a final balance of $904.69. Of this balance, his children Jane, Elizabeth, and Thomas received a total of $238.66 on March 20, 1826. His son Adam Weir received his share of $79.55 on March 22, 1826.

The document *(below)* shows the receipt of Samuel Robinson Weir's portion of his father's estate in the amount of $79.55 to close out the estate on March 22, 1826.

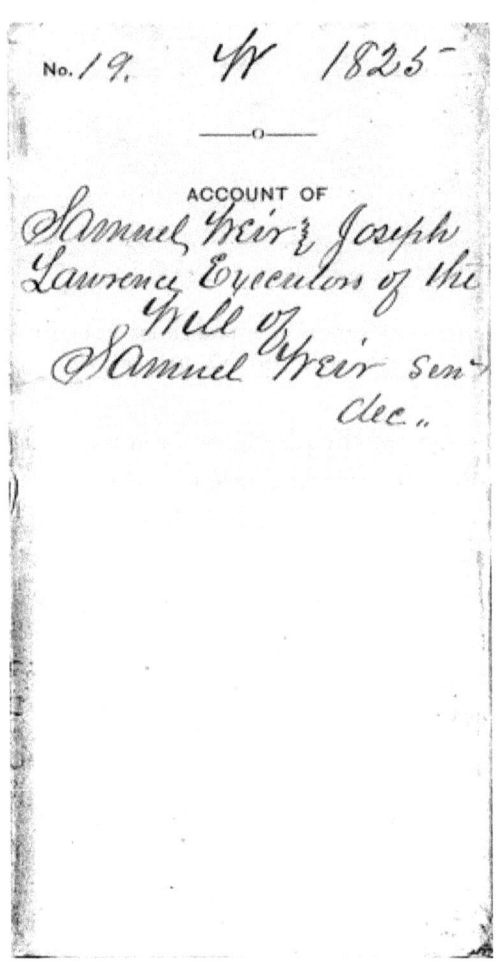

1825 Account of Samuel Weir and Joseph Lawrence

Will of Samuel) To all people to whom these presents may come or concern I Samuel
) Weir Senior of Washington County and State of Pennsylvania being in
Weir deceased) a tolerable state of health and of sound mind and understanding for
which I thank God and calling to mind the mortality of my body, that it is appointed for
man to die, do make and pronounce this my last Will and testament in form and manner
following) That is to say first and principally I commit my soul to God and my body
to the dust to be buried in a decent and genteel manner and as touching the worldly
substance God has bestowed on me I bequeath

WILL BOOK No. 3

as follows I give unto Adam Weir my son the plantation he now lives on, by him paying
unto Livina my daughter One hundred and six dollars and sixty seven cents immediately
after my executors hereinafter named execute unto him one good deed poll for the same
(which I authorize them so to do) I give unto Samuel my son the plantation I live on
now with the privilege of Livina to live with him on said plantation while she remains
single and the same he is not to sell without her consent until she is married I give
unto Livina my daughter one good mare saddle and Bridle I give unto Samuel my son the
Clock corner cupboard and the residue of the horse and creatures, all the rest of my
personal property including my outstanding debts to be equally divided between Samuel
my son and Livina my daughter excluding all the rest of my children but before and
distribution is made all my debts of whatever nature to be paid And I do hereby
nominate and appoint Samuel Weir my son and Joseph Lawrence Executors of this my Last
Will and testament. I testimony whereof I have hereunto set my hand and seal this tenth
day of October One thousand eight hundred and seventeen . Samuel X Weir (Seal)
his mark
Signed sealed and pronounced by Samuel Weir in presence of us who were present when
he signed Sealed and pronounced the same E Jenkins
James Erwin John Hartley

Washington County SS. Be it remembered that on the sixteenth day of April A. D. One
thousand eight hundred and twenty one before me Saml Lyon
Register for the probate of Wills and granting letters of Administration in and for
said County came Eleinas Jenkins and James Erwin the subscribing Witnesses to the
within last Will and Testament of Samuel Weir late of the County aforesaid dec'd who
being duly sworn do depose and say that they were personally present and did see the
testator therein named execute this will and did hear him publish pronounce and
declare the same to be his last will and testament, that at the time of his so doing
he was to the best of their apprehensions of sound and disposing mind memory and
understanding and that they respectively subscribed their names as witnesses to this
will in the presence of the testator and at his request and in the presence of each
other. E Jenkins

Sworn to and subscribed before me Saml Lyon. Register _____ James Erwin
1821. April 16th Letters Testamentary with copy of the Will and probate annexed
issued to Samuel Weir and Joseph Lawrence the Executors within named who on same day
were duly sworn. _____ Saml Lyon Register
Registered and compared with Original April 16th A. D. 1821

Will of Samuel Weir, Will Book #3
The will of Samuel Weir as per the Washington County Will Book 3, pages 411 and 412.

March 22, 1826, Document
Receipt of $79.55 to Samuel Weir for the portion of his father's estate.

LIFE ON THE FRONTIER

The Robinson families continued to live at the Big Sewickley Settlement during the 1780s. On November 8, 1786, Robert had 352 acres of land surveyed in Mount Pleasant Township, Westmoreland County. The warrant for the land was issued on August 24, 1786, and the patent was issued by Pennsylvania on May 14, 1788. This land was called "Salle."

In late 1785, apparently the oldest brother, William, talked his younger brother Robert into buying more land. This time it was in the wilderness of Armstrong Township, Westmoreland County, Pennsylvania, where William had approximately 200 acres that remained uncleared. On February 25, 1786, Robert was granted a warrant for 210¼ acres of land in Armstrong Township in Westmoreland County, Pennsylvania. The purchase price for the land was 3 pounds and 8 shillings of lawful money. The patent for the land was signed by Thomas Mifflin, Governor, and H. Irwin, Register. Robert had the 210¼ acres surveyed on April 22, 1787. This land would become known as "York." Shaped like a boot, the York lands overlooked the Kiskiminetas River. Here they would build a house and clear the land and would continue farming until 1820.

However, at the time of purchase, the York land was in the midst of numerous Native Americans and wild beasts and snakes. The country around was a howling wilderness, full of bears, wild cats, wolves, etc. No roads had been opened there except bridle paths, and the cabins of the pioneers were usually two to three miles apart.

The following description of the area is from the "History of the Presbyterian Church of Saltsburg, Penna." by the Rev. W. W. Woodend, dated 1870:

> From 1770 to 1794 there was much insecurity in the consequences of frequent attacks by the savages and the pioneers had often fled to safety to the older settlements. From time-to-time others accompanied them on their return and began new openings. Amongst the earliest families we have been able to trace distinctly, were the Wilsons, Wrays, Millers, Marshalls, Lemons, Pattons, Loves, Drums, Johnstons, Robinsons, Hendersons, McBrides, etc.

The land survey *(see document, p. 115)* shows the official survey dated "4th April 1787," of the land to be called "York."

+++

Although there were some settlers in Armstrong Township, Westmoreland County (today it is known as Conemaugh Township, Indiana County), shortly after the opening of the land office in 1769, the number was small. After the Revolutionary War began, most of these settlers abandoned their settlements and sought protection further southward nearer the rivers of Kiskiminetas and Conemaugh, some stopped in Ligonier Valley or returned to the east of the mountains. This condition continued until near the close of the war. At that time, some of those who had been driven off then returned, and other settlers came with them. After the close of the war, this section of the county became the "frontier," and there were various places intended for temporary refuge constructed out of the houses of the settlers at the time; but, while the apprehensions were great during the Indian Wars of 1790 and 1793, no serious depredations were committed by the few detached parties of Native Americans who lived in the region.

+++

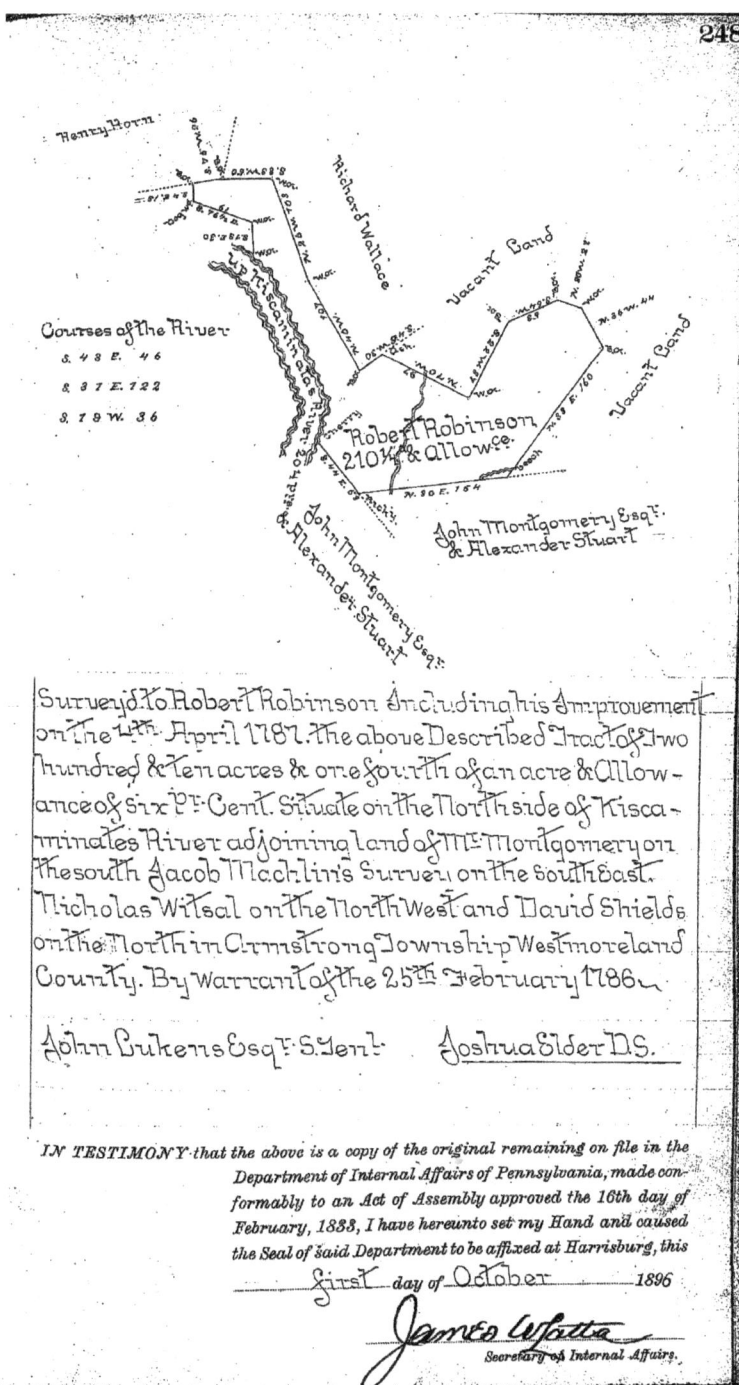

Robert Robinson Land, York Survey

A short time after getting the patent for the land, Robert and William made their way one mile north on the York lands (at the time there were no roads).

There they put up a hewed-log building, 24 feet by 28 feet, two stories high, and used it as a stockade. There were no windows or doors for a time. At the north end, 4 feet of the second log above the puncheon floor about the middle of the building was cut for an entrance in and out, and at night was barred from the inside. A puncheon floor was a plank or board made by hewing instead of sawing. American pioneers who could not procure the products of sawmills made much use of puncheons in their log buildings. This was a split log or heavy slab with the face smoothed. This building became known as the Robinson Strong House *(see story, pp. 123–126)*. Today, this fort is described and recognized as a "Frontier Fort" in Indiana County in western Pennsylvania.

Robert Robinson, 1786 Census

It was in this fort that they lived while they cleared the land, and for protection from the Native Americans while working there. When they returned to Mount Pleasant Township/Unity Township, they used the fort as storage for the tools and crops.

Meanwhile, Robert, his family, his brother William, and Margaret and her family continued to live in Mount Pleasant Township for the next few years while continuing to clear the land in Armstrong Township.

The 1786 Mount Pleasant Tax List showing that Robert had three horses, four cattle, and one sheep on 150 acres of land. The list also show that William was taxed for one horse.

Margaret Robinson had one horse, two, cattle and four sheep on 100 acres.

Name	Acres			
Rowley, Jn'o,	100			
Robertson, Marg't,	100	1	2	4
Rugh, Anth'y,	275	3	4	3
Robinson, Rob't,		2	2	
Raynor, Stophel,	100	1	2	3
Rankin, David,	300	2	3	2
Reasor, Fred'k,		1	1	
Robinson, Wm., single,		1		
Robinson, Rob't,	150	3	4	1
Robinson, Hugh,		1	1	2
Redleigh, Cha's,		1	1	
Ralston, Rob't,				
Rufinder, Simon,		1		
Robinson, And'w, single,				
Ryan, Geo.,		2	1	
Russell, Ja's,		2	2	2
Shaltzberger, Henry,		2	2	1
Speelman, Jn'o,	100	1	2	
Stockberger, Mathias,	100	2	2	4

1786 Mount Pleasant Tax List

Sometime between late 1788 and 1789, William moved to Armstrong Township, Westmoreland County, from the Big Sewickley Settlement and began living on the property that he purchased in 1773. This is known by the fact that the 1789 Return of Property in Armstrong Township, Westmoreland County, Pennsylvania, shows that William Robinson

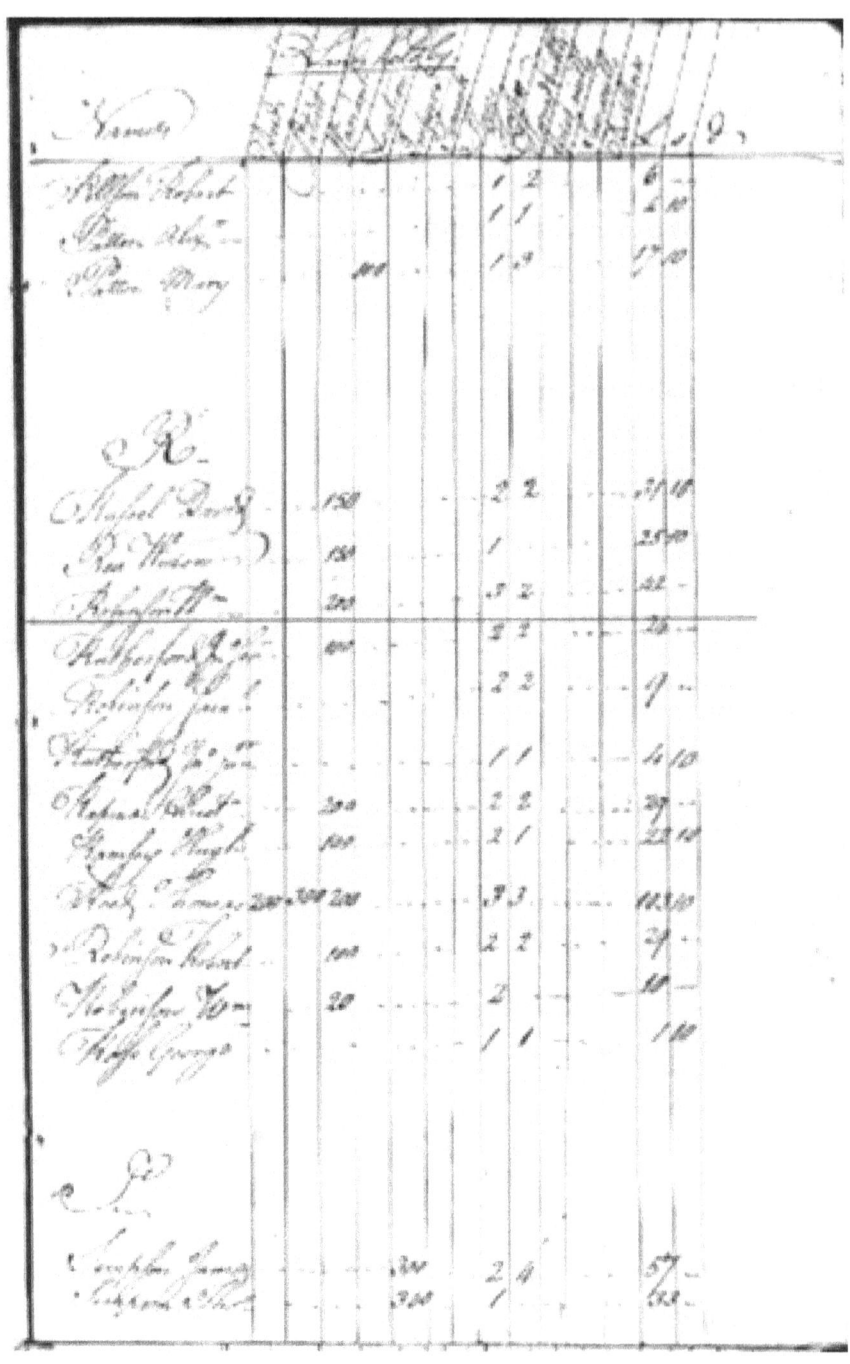

Tax List

finally had a plantation on the 200 acres with three horses and two cattle.

The same record shows Robert with 100 acres, two horses, and two cattle in Armstrong Township.

+++

Meanwhile, William's sibling Robert and his wife, Rachel, were still living at the Big Sewickley Settlement with their children. This is based on a record from the 1790 census of Westmoreland County, Pennsylvania, which shows that there were two adults and five children of Robert Robinson as registered in Unity Township, formerly Mount Pleasant Township.

1790 Census

While Robert purchased the York lands in 1786, they did not move to this location until 1794. There were several factors that delayed the move.

The biggest factor for not moving to Armstrong Township immediately after the purchase of the York lands was that Robert was appointed by the Orphans Court as the guardian of his brother's farm and children in Unity Township, Pennsylvania, after John's death. He took this responsibility seriously and mentored John's oldest son, Samuel, and would not leave the area until Samuel was twenty-one years old. Finally in 1793, all the property of his brother John's was legally turned over to John's oldest son, Samuel.

Another factor was that there was still a lot of insecurity in the territory in Armstrong Township. There were still frequent attacks by the Native Americans, and the lands were still full of bears, wild cats, and wolves, etc. It would not have been a safe place for a young family.

Later in 1794, with their three sons and two daughters, Robert and Rachel moved from the Big Sewickley Settlement to their plantation called York in Armstrong Township, Westmoreland County, near the mouth of Lick Run. They moved from the Big Sewickley Settlement on pack horses, crossing the Kiskiminetas River in a canoe, and floating their horses through the river. This was about a thirty-mile trek and would have taken about two to three days to travel. They settled on the north side of the river near the mouth of Lick Run, later to be known as Robinson Run, which flows into the Conemaugh River at the town of Edri. For the next twenty-six years, Robert Robinson and his family would live on the York lands in Armstrong Township, Westmoreland County.

His son James and James's wife, Mary Laughlin, lived with Robert and Rachel on the plantation. They helped with the chores and various work.

In 1803, Mary died, and soon after, in 1807, James died. Both were buried in the family burial ground called the Robinson River Hill Cemetery.

After James died, Robert found himself in a situation like that he experienced with the death of his brother John. In James' will dated July 9, 1807, James had purchased 300 acres of land *"conveyed by and instrument of writ bearing the date of 12th of October 1803 and signed by Jacob Wolf."* He bequeathed the 300 acres of land: 20 acres to his father, Robert, which were "opposite his front door"; 100 acres to his brother Capt. John; and 180 acres to his brother Robert S.

When James Robinson died in late November or early December 1807 without resolving the land dispute, his brothers, with the guidance of their father, Robert, were left to resolve the situation with Jacob Wolf.

+++

The following is the chronological timeline of documented events of the land dispute:

- » 1776, March 26 – A warrant was issued for 300 acres of the land to a Henry Hill.
- » 1786, March 22 – A warrant issued to Jacob Wolf to survey 300 acres,
- » 1788, June 22 – A survey was performed for 300 acres for Jacob Wolf, but according to later documents, he had not legally returned the survey to the Surveyor General Office.
- » 1828, March 11 – A survey was performed on the same 300 acres for Henry Hill based on the warrant issued on March 26, 1776. The survey was returned to the Surveyor General Office on the same day. The survey noted that the land in the Henry Hill survey warrant was previously surveyed and "appropriated" by Jacob Wolf in pursuance of a warrant dated March 22, 1786. In other words, Jacob Wolf had taken possession of the 300 acres without Henry Hill's authorization and was trying to get a patent to the land. Jacob Wolf then sold the 300 acres to James Robinson, knowing that he did not have a patent to the land and could not legally sell it.
- » 1829, June 20 – The 300 acres were resurveyed.
- » 1829, July 1 – A final patent was issued to the heirs of James Robinson from Jacob Wolf.

It took the Robinsons twenty-two years (1807–1829) to resolve this issue, and during that time Robert S. would become a county commissioner and sheriff and put political pressure on Jacob Wolf to correct the problem. Jacob Wolf eventually left Indiana County and moved to Armstrong County.

Robert would have been sixty-four years old when James died, and it would have been more difficult to work the 157 acres of the plantation by himself. But persevere he did, and Rachel and Robert continued onwards for the next seventeen years.

THE ROBINSON STRONG HOUSE

When Robert and William arrived at the York property in 1786, one of the first things they did was clear some land and build a safe house. This house would be simple and functional for the tasks at hand at that time. It would be two floors with no windows or doors. It would be used as a shelter when they were clearing the land, as a safe house against any marauders, and as a storage building for their tools and crops when they went back to the Big Sewickley Settlement.

What Robert and William didn't realize at the time was that this simple little building would become a historic symbol, not once but twice. First, the building became known as the Robinson Strong House and would serve as a historic fort on the Frontier. Second, after the threat of attacks by Native Americans vanished, the Robinson Strong House was used as the first school in the west or southwest corner of Indiana County. The small cabin was located three-fourths of a mile from the west corner of the county and a half-mile from the Kiskiminetas River. Students gathered for three hours in the evening, under the tutelage of James McDowell. Some of Robert's grandchildren would attend and learn to read and write, and eventually they would write about Robert and the family's history.

+++

The following excerpt is from the "Report of The Commission to Locate the Site of the Frontier Forts of Pennsylvania," Volume 2. Dated 1896, the Robinson's Strong House was noted as follows:

Robert Robinson with his family of 3 sons and 2 daughters, soon after 1780 moved from the Sewickley Settlement in Westmoreland County to the north side of the Kiskiminetas River near the mount of Lick Run, on lands call "York" in Conemaugh Township. In a short time, they made their way north one mile (no roads), put up a building twenty-four by twenty-eight feet, two stories high, and used it as a stockade. No windows or doors were there for a time. The second log from the puncheon floor had four feet of it cut out for an entrance. The building is still standing (1880), having been built nearly one hundred years. It is situated on part of the "York" lands.

Although the location of this house in a very dangerous part of the country, and the time of the erection one of great peril, there was no further account of it.

Information on the Robinson family and a description of the house built by Robert Robinson also can be found in *The Annals of Southwestern Pennsylvania, Vol. 2*:[1]

Robinson – One of the pioneers on the waters of Blacklegs Creek, in Conemaugh Township, was Robert Robinson, who formerly lived in the Sewickley Settlement, in Westmoreland County. He came from Sewickley, with a family of three sons and two daughters, about 1780, and recognizing that it was still Indian country north of the Kiskiminetas River, proceeded to make ample protection of his family and neighbors. He went upon the highlands overlooking the river, a few miles south of Fort Elder, and there built a log building, 24 feet long and 20 feet wide, two stories, with puncheon floors. It had no windows, but a four-foot entrance at one end. The fort stood for more than hundred years, but there is no record of an attack ever having been made upon it. The families of Fort Elder and Fort Robinson communities intermarried to for a substantial and God-fearing community, within which was the later the famous Elders Ridge Academy.

According to the book *Indiana County History* by J. A Stewart, the building was constructed for "perilous days."

> . . . *stations and blockhouses were kept up as security against the Native Americans. One was on a farm in Conemaugh Township owned by Robert Robinson called "Fallen Timber." The Robinson Strong-House was still standing in 1881, having been built nearly 100 years ago and then was looked upon as a relic of perilous days. It was located near the north line of the "York" lands. "Although the location of this house was in a very dangerous part of the country, and the time of its erection one of great peril, there is no further account of it.*

The following picture of the building on the site is of the school after it was rebuilt following a fire that destroyed the original building.

Robinson Country School, Near Nowrytown

The first school built in Conemaugh Twp., near Nowrytown, was Robinson #1 School which burned in 1917. The photo above of the school, rebuilt the same year, is from the album of Martin and Ethel Lynn, Conemaugh Twp.

Robinson School, First School in Conemaugh Township, Pennsylvania

The following map, dated 1880, shows the highlighted number +22 where the location of the Robinson Strong House was in Conemaugh Township, Indiana County, Pennsylvania.

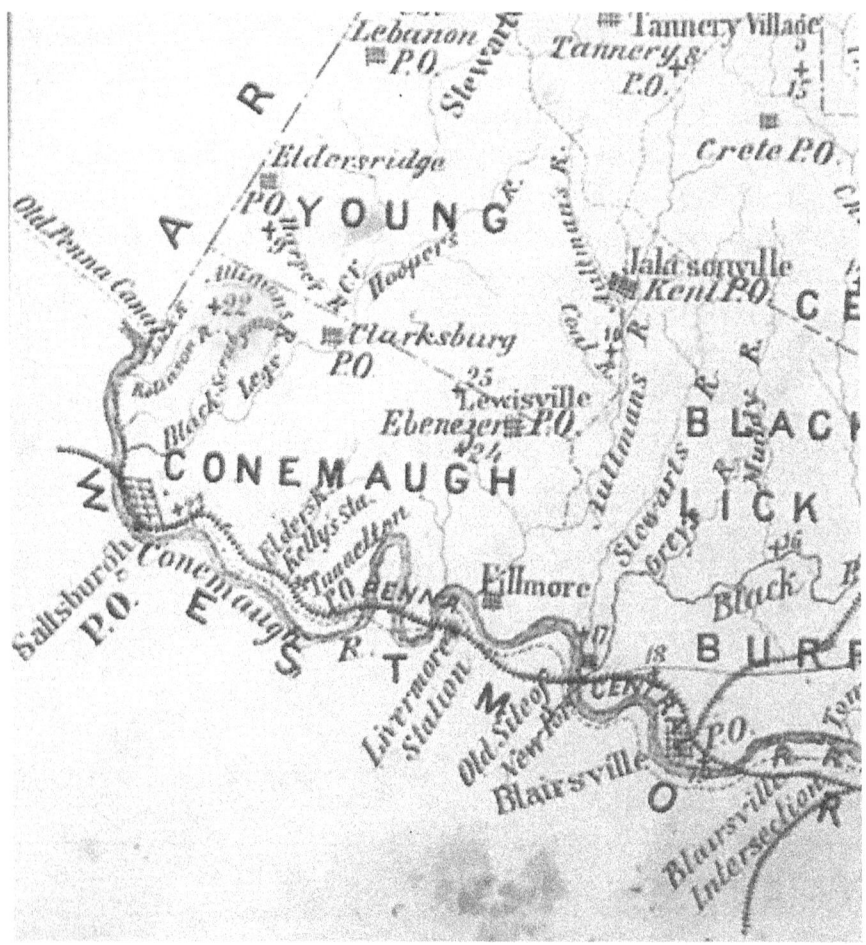

Robinson Strong House Location

A JOURNEY COMPLETED

Robert and Rachel continued to live on the York lands until 1820, when they went to their son Capt. John's home, which was a half-mile north on the "Iconium" lands. By this time Robert could no longer maintain their plantation, and Rachel's health was failing.

On Friday, October 31, 1823, Rachel died; she was in her eighty-fifth year. Robert was eighty-four years old at the time.

After Rachel died, the journey became Robert's to complete:

» On November 24, 1828, Robert sold the remaining 157 acres of York lands to his son Robert S.
» On November 11, 1829, Robert S. sold 150 acres to his older brother, Capt. John Robinson, for $500. The 20 acres that Robert was bequeath from his son James was given to Capt. John.*
» Robert S. and his wife, Elizabeth Black, lived on the remaining 7 acres of the York lands and continued to farm these lands until his death on November 17, 1833, at the age of fifty-three. Shortly after his death, his widow sold the plantation and moved to Saltsburg, Pennsylvania, where she lived until her death.

---

*The York property was sold in two segments. The first segment of 64-½ acres to Thomas Hindman and the second segment of 157 acres to Robert S. Robinson. This totals to 221-½ acres. The original York property was 210-¼ acres. However, the survey provides for a 6 percent margin of error. Therefore, the total amount of the York property was a maximum of 222 acres of land.

- » The remaining acreage of the York property was sold by Capt. John to his son Samuel S. Robinson. The land remained in the family until the heirs of Samuel sold the property to a William Kennedy on March 12, 1898.

The selling of the remaining property known as the York lands therefore ended the era of frontier life of the first two generations of the Robinson family.

+++

In March 1836, the family patriarch, Robert, was stricken with palsy. He died on Thursday, June 23, 1836, his ninety-seventh year. He spent the last sixteen years of his life living with his son, Capt. John. Both Robert and Rachel were buried on the family burial grounds, called the Robinson River Hill Cemetery.

"He sleeps besides his beloved partner."

Robert endured many deaths on this journey that took him from his birthplace in Northern Ireland to a new colony of British America, where he lived as one of the foundation citizens of the new United States of America. He experienced the deaths of many family members:

- » his father, Robert Senior, in 1771
- » his mother, Isabella, in 1771
- » his brother John in 1782
- » his brother William in 1799
- » his son James and James's wife in 1807 and 1803
- » his daughter Martha in 1812
- » his sister Lavina in 1818
- » his brother-in-law Samuel Weir in 1821
- » his wife, Rachel, in 1823
- » his son Robert in 1833
- » his sister Jennie's death between 1820 and 1825.

THE JOURNEY FORWARD

The following map shows the journey and timeline that the Robinson family traveled on the complete journey from their arrival in Philadelphia in 1770 to their final destination at the "York" lands in 1794.

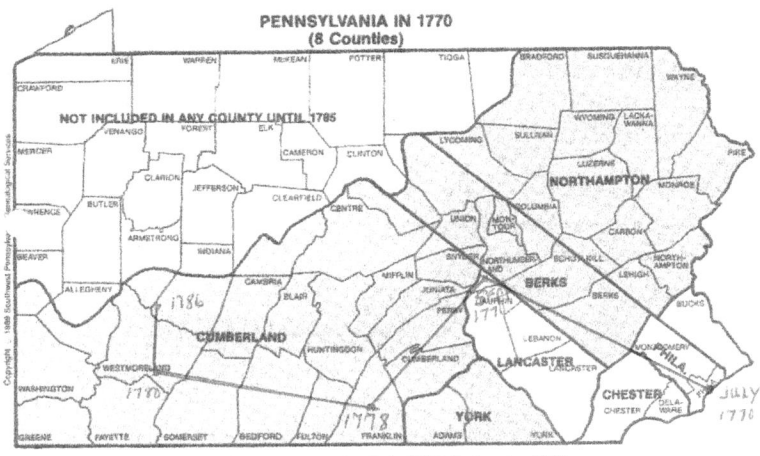

The Journey Map

If it was not for this family's determination, perseverance, fortitude, and strength to keep moving forward despite all the deaths, obstacles, and hardships along the way, then the ancestors would not be where they are today.

The following map *(see map, p. 130)* shows the legacy that the first and second generation of the Robinsons left in Indiana County, Pennsylvania. For the following generations, the influence of the Robinson family grew. The amount of property they owned increased and included an area of Indiana County that was named the "Robinson District."

This map, dated 1871, shows the location of the Robinson District in Conemaugh Township, Indiana County, Pennsylvania. It shows the location of the blockhouse called the Robinson Strong House, and the body of water called the Robinson Run and the Robinson River Hill Cemetery.

The Robinson Strong House was located on the Robinson property called York. The roads that are shown on the map are still in existence today. The road that it is located near the Robinson Strong House is today called Elders Ridge Road.

Additionally, the children of Robert S. Robinson, the youngest son of Robert Robinson, owned between eight and eleven buildings in the town of Saltsburg, Pennsylvania, in the mid to late 1800's.

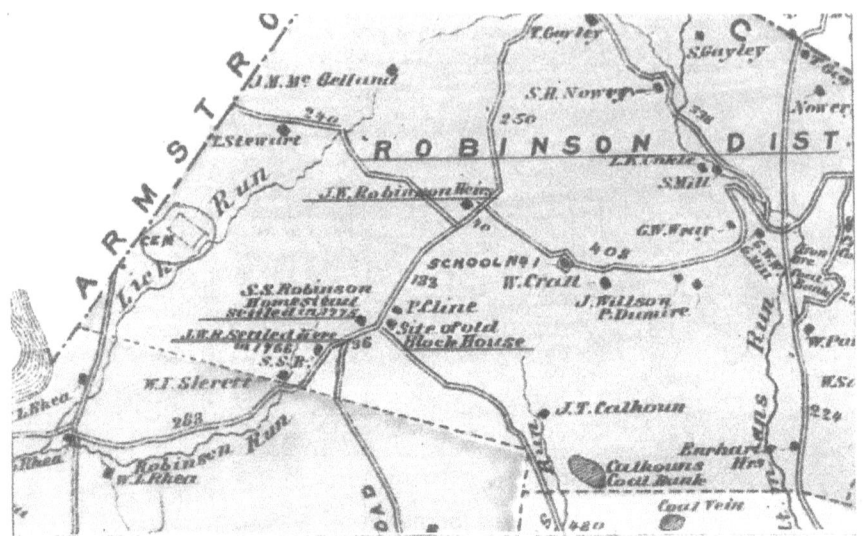

Robinson District Map

ROBINSON RIVER HILL CEMETERY

The Robinson River Hill Cemetery is the only remaining parcel of the land known as York. This is a .62 acre of land that is the family burial ground overlooking the Kiskiminetas River.

The Robinson River Hill Cemetery is in Conemaugh Township, Indiana County, Pennsylvania. The cemetery was established in 1794 on a small piece of York land owned by Robert Robinson.

In 1841, this cemetery became a multi-family burial ground and was then known as River Hill Cemetery. Sometime after 1882, the name was changed to Edri Cemetery.

The town of Edri arose as a coal mining town, formerly known as Coalport (1827–1882). Edri was located on the Old Main Line of the Pennsylvania Canal, north of Saltsburg and due east of Avonmore, Westmoreland County, and was along the banks of the Kiskiminetas River. The town of Edri is considered a ghost town, and the cemetery has been abandoned for quite some time.

This old cemetery is no longer used and has not had a burial for over 150 years. This land was originally deeded to Robert Robinson as part of the 210¼ acres warranted on February 25, 1786. It is in the southwestern portion of the original lands called York and overlooks the Kiskiminetas River on the western side of the property. The first burial occurred in September 1795 and continued until 1848.

On May 29, 1798, Robert and Rachel Robinson sold 64½ acres to Thomas Hindman for 50 pounds. Mistakenly, the burial grounds were included in the sale of the land, and it was not identified as a burial ground on any documents of the sale.

Thomas Hindman died May 29, 1803, and the land and all his assets were assigned to Jacob Frick, a local attorney. Frick was named the guardian of the estate since the law at the time was that Hindman's widow could not own the land and assets. All of Hindman's children were considered minor, and under the law at the time, the Orphans Court administered the estate of minors and incapacitated persons. If one parent passed away, the court would appoint a guardian to manage the estate even if the other parent was still living. The guardian would be responsible for the estate until the minor children became of age to inherit the estate.

Marker for Robinson River Hills Cemetery

To add to the confusion, the sale of the land in 1798 occurred in Armstrong Township, Westmoreland County; however, the deed was not recorded until January 17, 1807, in Conemaugh Township, Indiana County. (Indiana County was established in 1803.) The estate of Thomas Hindman was finally awarded, by inquest at the Orphans Court, to Jacob Frick on March 29, 1820.

Jacob Frick then proceeded to sell the land to William H. Richardson, on April 3, 1837. Upon discovery of the mistake of the burial ground parcel of land, Mr. Richardson sold the .62-acre parcel of land for $15 to Samuel Robinson (grandson of Robert Robinson), William Rhea, and Andrew Kier (son of David Kier, who is buried at this site). As a note of historical reference, Andrew Kier was the inventor of kerosene and later sold the patent to John D. Rockefeller. The cemetery was deeded on September 15, 1841, to a trust of Samuel Robinson, William Rhea, and Andrew Kier. It is assumed that the trust was for the perpetual care of the burial ground since there have been no further conveyances of this piece of property since 1841. At the burial ground the graves are marked with fieldstones that have no inscriptions or legible markings.

The only documentation available notes that there are four members of the Kier family and seven members of the Robinson family interred at the site. It is documented with the Sons of the Revolution that Revolutionary War Patriot, frontiersman, and pioneer Robert Robinson was buried at this site in 1836. He and his family were one of the original pioneers of Indiana County. Robert was the last of his family to be buried at this site.

The following was written by John M. Robinson, grandson of Robert Robinson, in 1880. This document provides proof that Robert Robinson has been buried at this site since 1836 and has not been moved.

> *The above grave-yard is located about one hundred rods (100) from the southwest corner of the county, on an elevation of two hundred (200) feet above the Kiskiminetas River. As the visitor turns his eye up the river then downstream, he beholds a beautiful curve in the river and as he looks over the river into Westmoreland County, nearly two hundred feet below him, a delightful loop of farms, upstream on the Indiana side, farms. As he turns his eye down the Indiana side into Armstrong County, an old Indian burial ground can be*

observed, and high bluffs. As the morning sun peeps over the horizon, it smiles on the same spot, and until the sun drops below the horizon the sight is grand to behold. In those sand mounds ten relatives of the writer repose. Forty-four years since the last relative was laid there. This was the only convenient place at that date (1836). Others of the first settlers sleep there.[2]

The photos *(below and next page)* are actual gravestones at the Robinson River Hill Cemetery. As shown, they do not identify who is buried at each location. It was common practice at the time to identify graves with fieldstones and no markings, since this was the frontier, and no engraving tradesman was available to mark the stones. All of the headstones face west overlooking the Kiskiminetas River. There are some footstones, and they are facing east. The headstones are grouped together closely, like a family, with the taller stones for the most important citizen and tiny stones for children. There is no standard height or width, although there is solid relationship between the importance of the deceased and the size of the head/foot stones.

Fieldstone Grave Marker

Fieldstone Grave Markers at Robinson River Hill Cemetery

EPILOGUE

> "Who lives, who dies, who tells your story?"
> —*Hamilton*, Lin-Manuel Miranda

THESE WORDS FROM THE FINALE SONG OF THE BROADWAY SHOW HAMILTON are fitting for anyone who desires to leave a legacy for those who follow. They are especially applicable to this story about a family named "Robinson."

The previous pages told the stories of the members of the first and second generations of the Robinson family that were then lost for so many generations.

The research of this story began a fantastic and sometimes awe-inspiring journey into the past that led to multiple books, a few memberships to the Sons of the American Revolution, a few memberships to the Daughters of the American Revolution, a ceremony commemorating a grandfather's military service with the placement of a headstone fifty years overdue, a partnership with a Pennsylvania cemetery for perpetual care of the markers for the descendants of the original ancestral family, and the discovery and restoration of the burial grounds (Robinson River Hill Cemetery) on the original York lands, which includes the historical resting place of the original Irish immigrant, Robert Robinson.

Upon completing the research of this journey, a long and rich history emerged encompassing significant historical events in America. These include the construction of the John Harris House, now known as the Cameron House in Harrisburg, Pennsylvania; participation by a number of family members as Patriots and Frontier Rangers during the American Revolutionary War; traveling to the western frontier on the historic Forbes

Trail; and living in and developing the frontier of western Pennsylvania, including the building of a frontier fort and even involvement in the Whiskey Rebellion of 1791–1794.

The Scots Irish Presbyterian settlers were considered hardy and sober citizens who recognized the value of education. One early historian described them collectively as *"a brave, determined, self-denying race, by no means deficient in education and love of learning. It is a notable fact that in spelling, penmanship, and accuracy of style and manner, the early records of the townships and county will compare favorably with those of more recent date."*

The Robinson family certainly lived memorable lives. In death, their stories were gradually forgotten. So, who will tell the story? The answer lies within these pages. We, as descendants, tell their stories within these pages. This book tells the stories of the lives of these amazing ancestors and how they lived and died, and it continues the tell the story of this family, picking up where Robert Robinson's grandsons left off in their documented family history dated 1881.

Even though, this is where the journey of Robert and Rachel Robinson ends, it is the beginning of the legacy of this branch of the Robinson family in America. The courage and fortitude exhibited during the journey by all the family members is inspirational. It's hard to imagine the life-changing decisions that were made during the journey—from first deciding to leave Ireland to moving west to the frontier with small children. In that time, they experienced the death of William's son on the ship, the death of their parents shortly after they arrived in British America, and the death of their brother John, who trailblazed their journey. But they kept moving forward. In the end, Robert outlived everyone that started with him on this journey, and even today, his legacy keeps moving forward.

There is a bit of irony in looking back, in that both John Robinson and his namesake, Capt. John, fell off their horses. John died, and Capt. John was never able to work again.

One question that remains: Why did Robert move his family to the York lands? He had an established plantation in a relatively safe area of the Big Sewickley Settlement. Why he would move approximately thirty miles north to clear 210 acres of land and rebuild his life, in his late forties to early fifties, in the wilderness remains unanswered. Was this decision somehow related to his brother's death? We will never know why, but by carving out his land and later establishing the "Robinson District," he put his mark on the family legacy. Maybe that was his vision for his family, one of creating an area that was notable on the frontier and living independently. Whatever the reason, the Robinson family was very prominent in this area of Indiana County, Pennsylvania, for several generations afterwards.

Endnotes

The Journey Part I
1. Page 7,"*These families remained...*" Robinson family document written in 1881 by the grandsons of Robert Robinson Jr.
2. Page 11, Phoenix Passenger List, July 25, 1770. Thomas Cadwalader, Cadwalader genealogical collection, "Passenger Lists, with Duties, August 29, 1768, to May 13, 1772," Philadelphia Customs House Records, Box 112, Folder 18, Historical Society of Pennsylvania, Philadelphia.

The American Revolutionary War
3. Page, 15, "Active service, when it occurred..." The Conestoga Area Historical Society article entitled "The Pennsylvania Militia." The Conestoga Area Historical Society article entitled "The Pennsylvania Militia."
4. Page 15, "Regardless of what they decided..." Journal of the American Revolution, Explaining Pennsylvania's Militia.
5. Page 15, "Occasionally, militia reinforcements..." Hay Genealogy for the Pennsylvania Militia.
6. Page 16, "He was thirty-seven years old." Pennsylvania Historical and Museum Commission and the Pennsylvania Archives, Fifth Series, Volume 7, pages 550–555.
7. Page 17, "His Washington County..." Pennsylvania Archives, Sixth Series, Volume 2, page 168.
8. Page 18, "After taking the Oath of Allegiance..."Pennsylvania Archives, Second Series, Volume XIII, page 453.
9. Page 20, "On the April 20, 1778, Muster Roll..." Document is from the Lancaster History Museum, Pennsylvania Records of the Office of the Comptroller [series #4.51], RG-4, Revolutionary War Associators, Line, Militia and Navy Account, and Misc. Records Relating to Military Service, 1775-1809, Subseries 3A, Militia Accounts, 1777-1794, 1-3261 box 24, Lancaster County, 1777-1780, 3rd Battalion, 2nd Company, Capt. Robinson [1 folder].
10. Page 23, John Robinson, Ranger Service. "Rangers on the Frontiers —1778-1783." Pennsylvania Archives 3rd Series, Volume 23, page 224.
11. Page 25, "After the battle of Brandywine..." Lancaster County History collections.
12. Page 26, Battle of Brandywine Map, https://www.battlefields.org/learn/maps/brandywine-september-11-1777.

The Big Sewickley Settlement
1. Page 39, "Payment of the 1783 taxes..." Pennsylvania Archives, Third Series, Volume XXIII, pages 435-436.

Their Stories
William & Jane
1. Page 46, "He had two horses …" Pennsylvania Archives Third Series, Volume 17.
2. Page 51, "William's Last Testament …" His will is documented in Book 1, page 153, #221, in Westmoreland County, Pennsylvania.

Robert Jr. & Rachel
1. Page 56, "James Elder was the oldest son …" Pennsylvania Library and Museum, certification dated March 14, 1929
2. Page 56, "During the American Revolutionary War …" Pennsylvania Library and Museum, certification dated March 14, 1929.
3. Page 60, "Sometime about October 1841 …" Pennsylvania Library and Museum, certification dated March 14, 1929.

John & Margaret
1. Page 66, She was the wife of …" The personal letter is from Francis Robinson Johnston to his grand nephew Hugh Raymond Johnston, dated March 18, 1898, in North Jackson, Mahoning County, Ohio.
2. Page 66, "Samuel Robinson is reported …" Genealogical and Personal History of the Allegheny Valley, Pennsylvania, under the editorial supervision of John W. Jordan. Vol. 3, page 892.
3. Page 66, "The death dates …" Register of Deaths, Slate Lick Presbyterian Church, Slate Lick, Armstrong County, Pennsylvania, p. 74 of transcript by DAR, Massy Harrison chapter, New Kensington, PA, 1960.
4. Page 69, "Then in spring of 1771 …" *The Jamesons in Pennsylvania.*
5. Page 69, "There is documentation …" William Edgar (1786) and John and James Edgar (1789) received warrants for land immediately to the east of the John and Margaret Robinson tract in Mount Pleasant Township/Unity Township. All three tracts are immediately north of Sewickley Manor land, thus indicating that this refers to the same John Robinson. Also Deed Book No. 2, page 100, indicates that Robert Taylor was a neighbor of the widow Margaret Robinson in 1794.
6. Page 70, "The Westmoreland County …" The Westmoreland Co. Orphans Court XOC, page 25.
7. Page 75, "Land Transfer from Margaret Robinson …" Source: LDS Family History film no. 0929166, Westmoreland Co. PA Deed Book No. 1, p. 380, 381.
8. Page 81, "The rollowing is the will …" Will Abstract in Old Westmoreland County, p. 14, Vol. 4, issue 4.
9. Page 82, "Missing from this sale …" Westmoreland Deed Book No. 8, pages 178–79.
10. Page 92, "The following is a summary …" Old Westmoreland, Vol. VI, No. 2, page 2. Deed Abstracts, Westmoreland County, Book 8-1.

11. Page 85, "The following is the original deed ..." Westmoreland Deed Book No. 8, pages 176–178).
12. Page 89, "This is based on ..." pa-roots.com/~Armstrong/taxables1807.html).
13. Page 98, "On June 13, 1810 ..." Armstrong Deed Book 4, p 95, recorded 24 April 1821, Margaret Peoples grantee, Samuel Robinson al grantor, Buff Twp.
14. Page 89, "The widow Margaret Peoples ..." http://www.pa-roots.com/~armstrong/census/1820arm3.html.
15. Page 89, "On March 3, 1821 ..." -- twp., recorded 3 Mar 1821, book 4, p 70.
16. Page 89, "The land is said to be part ..." Armstrong Deed Book 4, p 95, record 24 April 1821, Margaret Peoples grantee, Samuel Robinson al grantor, Buffalo Twp..
17. Page 90, "Then on April 7, 1833 ..." www.pa-roots.com/~armstrong/smith project/history/chap23.html Chapter 23 East Franklin – Smith Book.
18. Page 90, "Adjoining 'Lamie Bay' ..." Armstrong Co. PA Deed Book 10, Margaret Peoples to John Reed, Franklin Twp., recorded on 7 April 1837, vol. 10 page 309. Sold for trivial amount and agreement to keep Margaret Peoples in the future.

Lavina & Samuel
1. Page 96, "These families remained ..." October 1881 original source document entitled "Genealogy of the Robinson Family" as per John M. Robinson, son of John and Jane Marshall Robinson and grandson of Robert Robinson. Written by J. S. Elder, son of Martha Robinson Elder and daughter of Robert Robinson.

The Robinson Strong House
1. Page 124, "Information on the Robinson family ..." From the Annals of Southwestern Pennsylvania, Volume 2, Walkinshaw, Lewis Clark, New York: Lewis Historical Publishing Company, Inc. 1939, page 231.

A Journey Completed
1. Page 132–33, "The above graveyard ..." From the "Genealogy of the Robinson Family, Embracing six generations," from the History of Indiana County by J. A. Caldwell 1880).

About the Author

James Sagan proudly traces his maternal family roots through this story of the Robinson family, and their arrival to British America on July 25, 1770.

He was born and raised in the area where his ancestors settled and farmed on the western frontier and still, today, has family ties to these areas.

This is the third historical nonfiction book written by the author in this genre and referencing the Robinson family. The first book, *A Pioneer and Patriot* follows the life of Robert Robinson. The second book, *Our Robinson Legacy* is a genealogical story of the direct lineage of five generations.

www.ingramcontent.com/pod-product-compliance
Lightning Source LLC
Chambersburg PA
CBHW070851050426
42453CB00012B/2144